HURDLING

HURDLING

Malcolm Arnold

(National Athletics Coach, Wales)

First Edition   1952 by John Le Masurier
Second Edition   1954 by John Le Masurier
Third Edition   1966 by John Le Masurier
Reprinted   1972
Reprinted   1974
Reprinted   1979
Fourth Edition   1985 by Malcolm Arnold
This Edition   1992

ISBN 0 85134 107 1   3M/38M/01-92

© British Athletic Federation
Edgbaston House, 3 Duchess Place,
Birmingham B16 8NM

Typeset in Photina, printed on 115 gsm
Fineblade Cartridge and bound by
BPCC-Wheatons Ltd, Exeter

Contents

About the Author

Malcolm Arnold was the Director of Coaching in Uganda from April 1968 until December 1972. During that period he was responsible for the revival of Ugandan Athletics and coached John Akii-Bua to his gold medal and world record of 47.82s in the 400 metres hurdles in the 1972 Olympic Games.

In 1974 he became the National Coach for Wales. During his time in Wales he has coached many successful hurdlers and sprinters, including Nigel Walker [1984 Olympic hurdler], Kay Morley [1990 Commonwealth 100 metres hurdles champion] and Colin Jackson [World junior champion 1986, Olympic silver medallist 1988, Commonwealth and European champion 1990 and British, European and Commonwealth record holder]. He has been chief coach for the jumps, sprints and hurdles in the UK at various times since 1974 and is currently chief coach for sprints. He has been coach to many British teams, including the Olympic Teams of 1980, 1984 and 1988 and the World Championships Teams of 1983, 1987 and 1991. He particularly enjoys the task of training coaches at all levels in the UK, as well as the development of athletes' performance.

Acknowledgements

To all my athletes, especially those who through the years have helped me to a better understanding of hurdling.

To Stan Greenberg for supplying the statistics in the final section of the book.

Photographs

Cover photo of Colin Jackson [13.20s, Belfast 1990] by Mark Shearman.
Photo sequences by Howard Payne.
Other photos by Mark Shearman and Malcolm Arnold.

1 Introduction to Hurdling

The aim of this book is to inform coaches and athletes about up to date methods of preparation for hurdling at all levels.

It is very important that all young people in athletics "have a go" and are taught hurdling at an early age, preferably no later than their early 'teens. If at a later stage of development the sprinter or the middle distance runner decides to try hurdling or steeplechasing, then the groundwork of basic hurdling technique will have been learned.

Hurdling is a very enjoyable activity and encourages agility, co-ordination and fast running. It is a challenge to the athlete and a basic athletic requirement for a number of other athletic events.

A BRIEF HISTORY

It seems that hurdling began dangerously! It is believed that rough sheep hurdles were the basic equipment in the last century. Photographs of hurdlers competing in the first years of this century suggest that the hurdles were of very robust construction. Contact with these barriers was best avoided. Present day hurdling techniques demand that athletes clear the hurdles with a very close margin and more recent hurdle design allows this.

Men's sprint hurdling has been included in the Modern Olympics since 1896, but the Athens race was over 100 metres. Thereafter the race was standardised at 110 metres. 400 metres hurdles for men was included in the 1900 Olympics for the first time.

Women's sprint hurdling was run over various distances during the 1920's. In 1926 it was decided to standardise the distance at 80 metres over 8 flights and this event was first held in the 1932 Olympics. After the 1968 Olympics in Mexico City, the distance was increased to 100 metres hurdles over 10 flights. 400 metres hurdles for women is a relatively new event in major championship programmes. The first European Championship race was held in Prague in 1978. The first World Championship was contested in Sittard, Holland in 1980 and the first Olympic race took place in Los Angeles in 1984.

At the highest level, Britain has produced many outstanding hurdlers. Don Finlay won a bronze in the 1932 Olympics and a silver in the 1936 Olympics in the 110 metres hurdles. In the 400 metres hurdles, Leonard Tremeer won a bronze medal in 1908, Lord Burghley won a gold medal in 1928 and John Cooper won a silver medal in 1964. In 1968 in Mexico City, David Hemery won the gold medal with a world record time of 48.1 seconds. John Sherwood won the bronze in the same race. In 1972, David Hemery won a bronze medal and Gary Oakes won a bronze in Moscow in 1980. Hemery's British record stood until the European Championships in Split, Yugoslavia in 1990, when Kriss Akabusi won with a new record time of 47.92 seconds. He improved this record to 47.86 seconds in placing third at the 1991 World Championships in Tokyo.

Since 1985, there has been a tremendous upsurge in men's sprint hurdling in Britain. This was led by two Juniors, Jonathan Ridgeon and Colin Jackson. Ridgeon won the European Junior Championships in Cottbus, Germany in 1985 with a European junior record of 13.46 seconds, with Jackson second in 13.69 seconds. In 1986, Jackson won the World Junior title in 13.44 seconds, with Ridgeon second in 13.92 seconds. In 1987 in Rome, Ridgeon was second in the World Senior Championships, with Jackson third. In 1988, Jackson won the Olympic silver medal, Ridgeon was 5th and another outstanding young Briton, Tony Jarrett, was 6th. In 1990, Jackson won both the Commonwealth and European titles, with Tony Jarrett second in both races. In that year, Jackson was the world's fastest hurdler at 13.08 seconds, which is the present European record. In 1991 Jarrett won the bronze medal at the World Championships in Tokyo. In the wake of these three athletes, there are a number of other outstanding world class athletes in Britain.

Until recent times, British women's Olympic hurdling successes were confined to Maureen Gardner's silver medal in 1948 and Carol Quinton's silver medal in 1960, both in the 80 metres hurdles. In 1984 Shirley Strong won the silver medal in Los Angeles in 12.88 seconds. In 1990, Kay Morley won the Commonwealth 100 metres hurdles title with a Games record of 12.91 seconds. Sally Gunnell won the 400 metres hurdles at those Games, and then in 1991 took the silver medal at the World Championships.

HURDLING BASICS

Above all hurdlers who run over the sprint distances and the 300 and 400 metres hurdle must be fast sprinters. It is obviously desirable to have a good hurdle clearance technique, but speed *over and between the hurdles* is most important. The development of flat speed and limb speed must be encouraged in the learning and subsequent training processes.

Hurdlers must also be very supple, especially in the hip joints, the hamstrings and the lower spine. Fortunately, for athletes who are not naturally supple, concerted hard work can produce it quickly. As a general rule, women are more supple than men.

Running a hurdles race in balance is sometimes difficult. Athletes who are well co-ordinated and agile can handle the problems of balance quite adequately.

2   Races and Rules

This chapter embraces the more important aspects of rules relating to hurdling. As this manual is primarily directed to coaching, the rules outlined here are necessarily abbreviated. For a full description readers should purchase the current edition of the BAF handbook and/or the IAAF handbook.

When teaching hurdling, it is important to modify the event by changing the configuration of the hurdles. Hurdling should be made suitable to the athlete first, before any competition takes place. If hurdles are lowered and distances reduced, the learning process will become easier and quicker. When the time comes to compete the athletes must then conform to certain rules and regulations which stipulate the type of hurdles to be used, their height and the distances between.

THE CONSTRUCTION OF A HURDLE

Hurdles are very expensive items of equipment and must be cared for and meticulously maintained.

Wherever possible, an "International" type of hurdle should be used. A hurdle should consist of two uprights supporting a rectangular frame and should have a level and rounded top rail.

The total weight of the hurdle should be not less than 10 kilograms.

The extreme width shall be 1.20 metres and the extreme length of the base shall be 70 centimetres. The top rail shall be 70 centimetres in width and between 10 mm and 25 mm thick. The top rail shall be painted black and white.

DIAGRAM 1   EXAMPLE OF APPROVED HURDLE

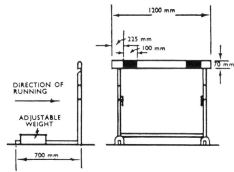

(adjustable weight may be inside or outside base)

TOPPLING FORCE

The hurdle must be so designed that a force of at least 3.6 kgs applied at the centre of the top of the cross bar is required to overturn it. When an adjustable hurdle is used, the counter weights (on the hurdle feet) must be adjustable to the effect that in every position the force required to overturn the hurdle, when adjusted, shall be at least 3.6 kgs and not more than 4 kgs. In races for Intermediates and Minors (of both sexes), Girls and Boys, the force required to overturn the hurdle shall be at least 2.7 kgs and not more than 3 kgs. The hurdles shall be so placed on the track that the ends carrying the uprights shall be farthest from, with the counterweights nearest to, the starting line.

Note:

In the training situation it is often sensible to make the toppling force as light as possible, so that the risk of injury is minimised, particularly when the athlete is fatigued.

KNOCKING DOWN THE HURDLES

Where hurdles are used which overturn with less force than the minimum specified, a competitor knocking down three or more hurdles shall be disqualified. This situation could arise in schools, where the International type of hurdle is not available.

If any athlete deliberately knocks down any type of hurdle, either by hand or foot, he shall be disqualified.

TRAILING

Competitors who trail a foot or leg below the top bar of the hurdle at the instant of clearance, or negotiate any hurdles not in their lane, shall be disqualified.

SPECIFICATIONS FOR HURDLES RACES
Outdoors

Distance of race	Height of hurdle	Distance to 1st flight	Distance be- tween flights	Distance to finish	Number of hurdles	Toppling weight
MEN'S EVENTS						
Seniors						
110m	106.7cm	13.72m	9.14m	14.02m	10	3.6kg
400m	91.4cm	45m	35m	40m	10	3.6kg
Juniors						
110m	99.0cm	13.72m	9.14m	14.02m	10	3.6kg
200m	76.2cm	18.29m	18.29m	17.1m	10	3.6kg
400m	91.4cm	45m	35m	40m	10	3.6kg
Intermediates						
100m	91.4cm	13m	8.5m	10.5m	10	2.7kg
400m	84.0cm	45m	35m	40m	10	2.7kg
Boys						
80m	84.0cm	12m	8m	12m	8	2.7kg
Minor Boys						
80m	76.2cm	12m	8m	12m	8	2.7kg
WOMEN'S EVENTS						
Seniors and Juniors						
100m	84.0cm	13m	8.5m	10.5m	10	3.6kg
400m	76.2cm	45m	35m	40m	10	3.6kg
Intermediates						
80m	76.2cm	12m	8m	12m	8	2.7kg
100m	76.2cm	13m	8.5m	10.5m	10	2.7kg
200m	76.2cm	16m	19m	13m	10	2.7kg
300m	76.2cm	50m	35m	40m	7	2.7kg
400m	76.2cm	45m	35m	40m	10	2.7kg
Girls						
75m	76.2cm	11.5m	7.5m	11m	8	2.7kg
Minor Girls						
70m	68.2cm	11m	7m	10m	8	2.7kg

VETERANS' EVENTS

Men 40–49

110m	99.0cm	13.72m	9.14m	14.02m	10	3.6kg
400m	91.4cm	45m	35m	40m	10	3.6kg

Men 50–59

100m	91.4cm	13m	8.50m	10.5m	10	3.6kg
400m	84.0cm	45m	35m	40m	10	2.7kg

Men 60–69

100m	84.0cm	13m	8.5m	10.5m	10	2.7kg
300m	76.2cm	50m	35m	40m	7	2.7kg

Men 70 and over

80m	76.2cm	12m	7m	19m	8	2.7kg
300m	76.2cm	50m	35m	40m	7	2.7kg

Women 35–39

100m	84.0cm	13m	8.5m	10.5m	10	3.6kg
400m	76.2cm	45m	35m	40m	10	3.6kg

Women 40–49

80m	76.2cm	12m	8m	12m	8	2.7kg
400m	76.2cm	45m	35m	40m	10	2.7kg

Women 50 and over

80m	76.2cm	12m	7m	19m	8	2.7kg
300m	76.2cm	50m	35m	40m	7	2.7kg

NOTE: *In each case there shall be a tolerance of 3mm above and below the standard height to allow for variation in manufacture.*

Indoors

MEN'S EVENTS

Seniors

50m	106.7cm	13.72m	9.14m	8.86m	4	3.6kg
60m	106.7cm	13.72m	9.14m	9.72m	5	3.6kg

Juniors

60m	99.0cm	13.72m	9.14m	9.72m	5	3.6kg

Intermediates

60m	91.4cm	13m	8.5m	13m	5	2.7kg

WOMEN'S EVENTS

Seniors and Juniors

50m	84.0cm	13m	8.5m	11.5m	4	3.6kg
60m	84.0cm	13m	8.5m	13m	5	3.6kg

Intermediates

60m 'A'	76.2cm	12m	8m	16m	5	2.7kg
60m 'B'	76.2cm	13m	8.5m	13m	5	2.7kg

Girls

60m	76.2cm	11.5m	7.5m	18.5m	5	2.7kg

NOTE: *The above specifications appeared in the official Handbook for 1991/92. Check that there have been no subsequent changes!*

Those concerned with younger age groups can also seek advice from their relevant Schools' Association.

English Schools' AA   Mr N. Dickinson
22 Coniscliffe Road,
Stanley, Co. Durham,
DH9 7RF

Scottish Schools' AA Mr A. Jack,
11 Muirfield Street,
Kirkcaldy, Fife,
KY2 6SY

Ulster Schools' AA   Mr R. G. Moffett,
Belfast Royal Academy,
Cliftonville Road,
Belfast, BT14 6JL

Welsh Schools' AA   Mr D. J. Phillips,
Neuadd Wen,
Dol Llys Road,
Llanidloes, Powys,
SY18 6JA

3 The Technique of Hurdling

In hurdling there are constants and variables.

The constants are:
1 The distance from the start line to hurdle 1
2 The distance between hurdles
3 The height of the hurdles

The variables are:
1 The speed, strength and suppleness of an athlete
2 The physical build of the athlete (i.e. overall height, length of inside leg, height of centre of gravity)
3 The specific hurdling fitness of the athlete
4 The nature of the track surface
5 The direction of the wind
6 The nature of the competition (e.g. easy or hard race, qualifying round, major final etc.)

It is important to understand the relationship between these constants and variables. Inevitably a compromise is made between the two. Some athletes, because of their physical stature, "fit" the dimensions of a sprint hurdle event exactly. Others may have legs that are too long, whilst others will have legs that are too short. According to the degree of compromise to be made, the teacher or coach should vary the methods of preparation.

In considering women's sprint hurdling, especially at club level and above, there need not be too much compromise because:
1 STRIDE LENGTH between the hurdles relates more naturally to their normal sprinting stride length.
2 The PATH OF THE CENTRE OF GRAVITY need not be raised unduly during hurdle clearance, because of the relatively low height of the hurdle. When observing hurdlers side on, the top of the hip or shorts is a good rough guide for the path of the centre of gravity.

Related to the latter point, some authorities have argued that the height of women's hurdles should be raised to 91.4 cms (three feet). This would bring the challenge of their sprint hurdles event more into line with the men's event.

In considering the men's sprint hurdle event, there is a greater degree of compromise because:
1 STRIDE LENGTH Their stride length between hurdles does not closely relate to sprinting stride length.
2 The PATH OF THE CENTRE OF GRAVITY The athlete must raise his centre of gravity higher during hurdle clearance than he does in a normal sprinting stride.

It can be seen that the dimensions of the event are not absolutely constant, but change according to an athlete's structure and ability. The compromise between constants and variables is always present. Consequently, *there is not just one prescribed technique for sprint hurdlers*. The stature and ability of the athlete and the dimensions of the event are the final determinants of technique.

Life can sometimes be very difficult for young athletes as they move up their age groups. As an example, probably the most difficult transition is for young male hurdlers moving from the Youth group (15–17 years, 100 metres hurdles at 3 feet, with 8.5 metre gaps) to the Euro Junior group (17–20 years, 110 metres hurdles at 3 feet 6 inches, with 9.14 metre gaps). This transition demands such a complete change of technique that some coaches ask their athletes to regard the change as a transfer to a different event!

Because of these differences, the differential between flat sprinting times and hurdling times is difficult to estimate. However, this differential, at world level is suggested as being:

MEN   1.8 to 2.0 seconds
WOMEN   0.9 to 1.2 seconds

For athletes at school and club level this differential will be greater.

Similarly, there is a differential between an athlete's flat 400 metres time and his 400 metres hurdles time. This can be as low as 1.5 seconds for the world class athlete, but as high as 6 or 7 seconds for the beginner.

Successful hurdlers must be fast sprinters, so teachers and coaches of hurdling are tapping the same reservoir of talent as the sprints and jumps coaches! *It is difficult, if not impossible, to make a very fast hurdler from a very slow sprinter.*

SPRINT HURDLING
Stride Patterns

In successful sprint hurdling, there must be conformity to a stride pattern.

Eight strides are taken from the start to the first hurdle. There are some athletes who can take seven strides to the first hurdle, but they are exceptionally strong or have very long legs. This can happen in some of the younger age groups, as well as in the senior ranks. Unfortunately with a seven stride approach, the starting blocks have to be very close to the start line, which results in a bunched and uncomfortable starting position. Also, there has to be a considerable cadence (leg speed) change between the run to the first hurdle and the running between subsequent hurdles. If at all possible, it is best to have an eight stride approach which produces a cadence more equal to the three stride rhythm between the hurdles.

The three stride rhythm is absolutely necessary for fast times. Some club athletes, who find it difficult to reach with three strides, "change down" to four strides between

hurdles towards the end of the race. This requires an ability to take off and lead over the hurdle with either leg.

From the last hurdle to the finish, women usually take $4\frac{1}{2}$ to $5\frac{1}{2}$ strides and men 6 strides. Athletes should be made aware of this final part of the race, where it is often won or lost. The timing of the dip finish can mean the difference between success and failure.

The Anatomy of a Sprint Hurdles Race
The Start

The rules and starting commands for hurdling are exactly the same as for sprinting. A good basic position to start from is called the "medium" start. The "on your marks" and "set" positions are demonstrated by Colin Jackson in figures 1 and 2.

In the medium start, with the athlete in the "on your marks" position, the front foot is some 40–50 cms from the start line. The feet, in the starting blocks, are approximately shin length apart. In the "set" position, the hips are raised so that they are slightly higher than the shoulders. In turn, the shoulders should be above the start line. The head should be held in natural alignment with the spine.

A good check for a proper "set" position is to look at the angle behind each knee. The angle behind the front knee should be 90 degrees and behind the rear knee 120 degrees (see figure 2). The distance between the front foot and the back foot is about shin length.

Recent experience has shown that many athletes use a block spacing closer than the "medium" one. However it is sensible to begin with the "medium" setting and then experiment with closer block settings. The ultimate aim is to find the most efficient and comfortable set position an athlete can launch himself from. Figures 3 and 4 illustrate a closer block setting, currently used by 13.51 second hurdler Nigel Walker.

Fig. 1

Fig. 2

Fig. 3

Fig. 4

Experimenting with Block Positions

Hurdlers need to experiment with block positions. This enables them to find the most efficient approach run to hurdle 1.

Very often, hurdlers find that their natural stride length brings them too close to hurdle 1 with the eight stride approach, whereas a seven stride approach causes them to overstride and miss the correct take-off place. One solution to this problem would be to move the front block away from the starting line, effectively reducing the length of the first stride. This should have the desired effect of accommodating the eight-stride pattern. This is the type of problem athlete and coach might encounter during the competitive season.

Postural Changes in the Approach to Hurdle 1

Hurdles coaches must note that there is a big difference between a sprint start and a sprint hurdles start. Because the first hurdle is placed seven or eight strides from the start, the hurdler comes upright quite quickly after the gun is fired. In comparison the sprinter is encouraged to stay low for at least 10 strides.

The hurdler should think about sighting the hurdle after four strides, in readiness for the first clearance. This requires a much earlier rise towards an upright posture as compared with the sprinter.

When coming upright, the hurdler must also think of keeping the hips high, especially as he drives into the take-off for the first hurdle.

Stride Lengths in the Approach Run

Diagram 2 illustrates the approximate stride lengths for both the women's and men's events. It can be seen that stride lengths increase progressively until the seventh stride. The eighth stride is shorter, which allows the realignment of the hips ready for the hurdle take-off and clearance. Particular attention must be paid to the posture in the final stride where the stride length shortens, the trunk dips, but the hips must remain high. If the hips sink, a bad take-off will result, followed by a poor clearance.

Take-off and Landing Distances at each Hurdle during a Race

The take-off distance at each hurdle will vary according to factors such as speed of approach, height of hurdle and the length and speed of the leading leg. The usual take-off distance for a man will be 2m–2.3m from the hurdle base. On landing the foot will be 1.2m to 1.4m from the hurdle base (diagram 3). For women the take-off distance will be around 2m and the landing distance between 1m and 1.2m. *These measurements will vary according to the stage of the race*, because a sprint hurdler accelerates rapidly up to hurdle 3, holds speed for as long as possible, then decelerates towards the end of the race as he fatigues. As approach speed to the hurdle increases, take-off distances increase and landing distances decrease. As speed reduces towards the end of a race, take-off distances shorten and landing distances lengthen. So, as a sprint hurdles race progresses, ratios of take-off distance to landing distance change, but the overall distance cleared apparently remains the same.

Stride Lengths between Hurdles

Diagram 3 illustrates typical stride lengths between hurdles for men. The same ratios are applicable to the women's event. Note the length of the first stride off the hurdle, where

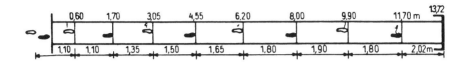

Mens' 110m Hurdles

Womens' 100m Hurdles

DIAGRAM 2.
Stride lengths in the approach to the first hurdle (from "Grundlagen der Leichtathletik"—Bauersfeld and Schröter).

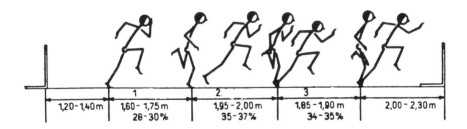

DIAGRAM 3.
Stride lengths of the three stride rhythm between 110m hurdles (from "Grundlagen der Leichtathletik"—Bauersfeld and Schröter).

11

the aim is to return quickly to a sprint rhythm. The second stride is the longest and the third stride is a preparation for another take-off, where the foot again moves quickly beneath the hips.

Sprint Hurdles Clearance

The clearance is typified by the shortening of the last stride by several centimetres, thus moving the foot quickly beneath the hips. An effective drive can then be made across the hurdle.

Many coaches demand an exaggerated lean, a trunk dip over the hurdle. However, the extent of the trunk dip depends on the height of the hurdler's centre of gravity and the height of the hurdle. Generally women clear the hurdles with a more upright trunk position. Compare photo CJ8 with photo KM5 (see end pages).

As a general rule, tall hurdlers running over low hurdles have an upright posture, whilst shorter hurdlers running over higher hurdles have an exaggerated forward trunk lean. This forward dip helps flatten the path of a hurdler's centre of gravity over the hurdle, so producing a more efficient hurdles clearance and a smooth transition into the running stride after the hurdle.

The Leading Leg

From a side-on observation position, the leading leg is picked up as fast as possible, bent at the knee (photos CJ4 and KM4). This flexion of the knee, and the ankle, causes the fast "pick-up" and allows the athlete to get closer to the hurdle during take-off.

From a head-on or rear observation position, the leg is picked up parallel to the lines on the track.

From the side-on position, once the knee of the leading leg approaches barrier height, the heel is thrust vigorously forwards (photos CJ5 and 6 and KM4 and 5). As the heel goes past the

barrier, the aim is to get the leading foot back to the ground as soon as possible (photos CJ8 to 12 and KM 5 to 7). On landing, the athlete must be in balance, with the body weight over the landing foot (photos CJ14 and 15 and KM7).

The Trailing Leg

As the leading leg is driving at the hurdle top, the trailing leg is still in contact with the ground, driving the body at the hurdle (photos CJ3 to 5 and KM4). As it leaves the ground, it folds and moves laterally to effect an efficient clearance (photos CJ5 to 10 and KM4 to 6). This action can be observed from three angles: the rear, the side and head-on. During the action, the hurdler must feel that the knee of the trailing leg is "pulling the foot through" in a very active manner, with the foot close to the buttock. The knee must continue through very high, to enable the stride off the hurdle to be both brisk and complete (photos CJ12–15 and KM6 and 7).

As the trailing leg crosses the hurdle, the foot must be "cocked" (everted) at the ankle, so that neither the toes nor the ankle itself hits the hurdle. If the trailing foot hits the hurdle at this point, the error will be costly (and painful!).

The knee of the trailing leg must cross the barrier at the same moment as the hip crosses it. When viewed from the side, the thigh of the trailing leg should be parallel to the barrier.

With some hurdlers, the knee of the trailing leg can cross the barrier before the hip. This can be caused by a slow leading leg, thrown up straight instead of bent at the knee. Athletes should be encouraged to throw the leg up bent at the knee and thus faster.

During barrier clearance the action of the trail leg is continuous. The downward/backward movement of the leading leg, complemented by the fast lateral recovery of the trailing leg, must be emphasised. The stride following the landing is the shortest and quickest and great emphasis should be placed on this during technical training.

Arm Actions

The arms work harmoniously with the legs and should act as opposites. They balance the hurdling action and help to absorb the tremendous thrust of the legs during driving phases.

As the lead leg rises, so the opposite arm goes out adjacent to the leg [photos CJ3 to 7 and KM4 and 5]. In women's hurdling there is often a marked cross body action [photos KM4 and 5].

As the lead leg begins its downward path to its landing, so the lead arm sweeps back wide, matching the timing of the leg [photos CJ10–13].

As the trail leg is driving the body at the hurdle, so the opposite arm drives back [photos CJ3 and 4]. As the trail leg passes forward over the hurdle towards its landing, so the opposite arm drives forwards.

Throughout the clearance the arms synchronise with the legs, and sprinting action should be resumed during the three strides between the hurdles.

The double arm shift, demonstrated by some athletes, where both arms go forwards as the leading leg is raised at take-off, is not recommended. This technique requires one arm to be shifted out of normal phase, thus causing speed loss. It is technically difficult and mechanically unsound.

At all times, shoulders and hips should remain square to the hurdle top bar. Emphasis should be placed on carrying the hips high throughout the race. If the hips are allowed to rise and sink unduly, particularly during take-offs and landings, hurdling speed and balance will be lost.

Towards the End of the Race

In top class races athletes are seen to accelerate most rapidly up to hurdle 2. They continue to accelerate up to hurdle 7 or 8. After that point, when the energy supply system begins to slow down and the muscles begin to lose their co-ordination, the athlete decelerates.

From hurdle 10 to the finish there is a second acceleration phase over the last 5 or 6 running strides, when the hurdler becomes a pure sprinter. The athlete should know how many strides there are from hurdle 10 to the finish and practise the run-in. Encourage athletes to run like sprinters to the finish. Experienced athletes should learn a "dip" finish. A well timed dip can win a race, but a badly timed dip can lose a race.

Patterns of a Race

Table 1 indicates the intermediate touchdown times one can expect in men's 110 metres hurdles races run at various speeds from 13.2 to 16.0 seconds.

Table 2 shows the same indicators for women's 100 metres hurdles run at various speeds from 12.3 to 15.0 seconds.

Table 3 shows the actual times of Kingdom, Jackson, Campbell and Jarrett in the 1988 Olympic Games men's final in Seoul. Table 4 shows the touch down times of Donkova, Siebert and Zacziewicz in the women's final and of Skeete, the best British woman in those Games. In these charts, the time of each athlete as he/she touches the ground after each hurdle is shown, followed by the time taken between each touchdown.

400 METRES HURDLES

The 400 metre hurdler needs a number of high degree skills. Some are the same as sprint hurdles skills but many are different. In the past the very best 400 metres hurdlers, especially the men, started their careers as sprint hurdlers. Towards the conclusion of this race there is a high degree of fatigue. Special abilities and training methods are required to cope with this part of the race. Good sprinters/hurdlers who have a good endurance capacity will do

13

TABLE 1

Time at Landing after	13.2–13.5	13.5–14.0	14.0–14.5	14.5–15.0	15.0–15.5	15.5–16.0
1st hurdle	2.4	2.4	2.5	2.6	2.6	2.7
2nd hurdle	3.4	3.5	3.6	3.7	3.8	3.9
3rd hurdle	4.4–4.5	4.6	4.7–4.8	4.9	5.0	5.1
4th hurdle	5.4–5.5	5.7	5.8–5.9	6.0	6.2	6.4
5th hurdle	6.4–6.6	6.8	6.9–7.1	7.2	7.4	7.6
6th hurdle	7.4–7.6	7.9	8.0–8.3	8.3	8.6	8.8
7th hurdle	8.5–8.7	9.0	9.1–9.4	9.5	9.8	10.1
8th hurdle	9.6–9.8	10.1	10.2–10.6	10.7	11.0	11.3
9th hurdle	10.7–10.9	11.2	11.3–11.8	11.9	12.3	12.6
10th hurdle	11.8–12.1	12.4	12.5–13.0	13.1	13.6	14.0
Finish line	13.2–13.5	13.5–14.0	14.0–14.5	14.5–15.0	15.0–15.5	15.5–16.0

SPLIT TIME CHART—110 METRES HURDLES.
From: "The Hurdle Races" by K. O. Bosen.

TABLE 2

Time at Landing after	12.0–12.5	12.5–13.0	13.0–13.5	13.5–14.0	14.0–14.5	14.5–15.0
1st hurdle	2.1	2.1	2.2	2.3	2.3	2.3
2nd hurdle	3.1	3.2	3.3	3.3	3.5	3.5
3rd hurdle	4.1	4.2	4.4	4.5	4.7	4.8
4th hurdle	5.1	5.3	5.5	5.6	5.9	6.0
5th hurdle	6.1	6.3	6.6	6.8	7.1	7.3
6th hurdle	7.1	7.4	7.7	7.9	8.3	8.5
7th hurdle	8.1	8.4	8.8	9.1	9.5	9.8
8th hurdle	9.1	9.5	9.9	10.2	10.7	11.0
9th hurdle	10.2	10.6	11.0	11.4	11.9	12.3
10th hurdle	11.3	11.7	12.1–12.2	12.6–12.7	13.1	13.5–13.6
Finish line	12.3	12.8	13.2–13.3	13.7–13.8	14.3	14.8–15.0

SPLIT TIME CHART—WOMENS 100 METRES HURDLES.
From: "The Hurdle Races" by K. O. Bosen.

TABLE 3

NAME		KINGDOM	JACKSON	CAMPBELL	JARRETT
PLACING		1st	2nd	3rd	6th
H1		2.55	2.57	2.60	2.58
		1.05	1.04	1.06	1.07
H2		3.60	3.61	3.66	3.61
		1.01	1.04	1.03	1.08
H3		4.61	4.65	4.69	4.73
		1.00	1.02	1.00	1.04
H4		5.61	5.67	5.69	5.73
		1.00	1.03	1.00	1.07
H5		6.61	6.70	6.69	6.84
		0.98	1.02	1.02	1.05
H6		7.59	7.72	7.71	7.89
		1.00	1.03	1.02	1.04
H7		8.59	8.75	8.73	8.93
		1.00	1.04	1.05	1.06
H8		9.59	9.79	9.78	9.99
		1.03	1.03	1.05	1.06
H9		10.62	10.82	10.83	11.05
		1.02	1.05	1.12	1.10
H10		11.64	11.87	11.95	12.15
H10 to finish		1.34	1.41	1.43	1.39
TIME		12.98	13.28	13.38	13.54

Wind speed + 1.50 m/s

TABLE 4

NAME	DONKOVA	SIEBERT	ZACZIEWICZ	SKEETE (s/f)
PLACING	1st	2nd	3rd	6th
H1	2.54	2.60	2.59	2.64
	1.01	1.01	1.02	1.05
H2	3.55	3.52	3.55	3.69
	0.97	1.01	1.01	1.06
H3	4.52	4.62	4.62	4.75
	0.98	0.96	0.97	1.02
H4	5.50	5.58	5.59	5.77
	0.96	0.96	0.99	1.04
H5	6.46	6.54	6.58	7.82
	0.96	0.96	1.00	1.01
H6	7.42	7.50	7.58	7.82
	0.96	0.96	1.01	1.03
H7	8.38	8.46	8.59	8.85
	0.96	1.00	0.99	1.04
H8	9.34	9.46	9.58	9.89
	0.97	1.00	1.01	1.08
H9	10.31	10.46	10.59	10.97
	1.01	1.00	1.03	1.08
H10	11.32	11.46	11.62	12.05
H10 to finish	1.06	1.15	1.13	1.18
TIME	12.38s	12.61s	12.75s	13.23s

Wind speed + .20 m/s [+ .50 m/s]

well in this event. Athletes who move from either sprint hurdling or 400 metre running to 400 metres hurdling must be initially patient, because they will need to learn a new "trade". This learning period could last as long as two years before full potential is realised.

Technique for 400 Metres Hurdles

The technique for sprint hurdles is relevant to 400 metres hurdles, although there are two major differences.

1 Relatively speaking, the hurdles are lower for 400 metre hurdlers and further apart. Thus the hurdling task is easier.
BUT
2 In 400 metres hurdles there is much more fatigue than in sprint hurdling and the training process must take account of this.

It is advisable for 400 metres hurdlers to practise all sprint hurdlers' drills as well as their own specific drills.

The photosequence of Kriss Akabusi (KA1 to 14—see end pages) show an excellently learned technique. Kriss was an outstanding 400 metre runner before changing to 400 metres hurdles late in his career. After two years solid work on hurdling and drilling, his technique was good enough to take him to a British record.

The photosequence of Sally Gunnell (SG1 to 12) show the technique of Britain's best ever lady hurdler. Sally holds the British record for sprint hurdles and 400 metres hurdles.

Stride Patterns

The greatest technical problems are concerned with stride patterns. Many athletes note the stride patterns used by world record holders or national record holders and feel that these are their targets. All athletes, beginner, novice or international, will have their own ideal pattern, based upon their speed and technical ability. Their stride patterns will change depending upon track or weather conditions. They will improve with better fitness for the event and with experience. For efficient, fast hurdling, stride patterns must be planned and practised.

Table 5 suggests a range of stride patterns adopted by hurdlers at various levels of performance and represents a good starting point.

It should be noted that an even number of strides demands that an athlete should ALTERNATE—so that he must be equally good at using the left or the right leg as the leading leg. This ability is essential and young athletes should be encouraged to alternate when they first learn to hurdle. They should then develop the skills with specific alternating drills and activities.

It also helps if the athlete can lead with the left leg around bends. When leading with the left leg around a bend there is a natural inclination to lean to the inside of the bend and this produces better balanced running into and away from the hurdle. Figures 5 and 6 show the athlete leading with the right and left legs. The postural differences can clearly be seen.

Table 6 gives examples of actual stride patterns used in races. *Everything else being equal,* the athlete who uses fewest strides during a race will be quickest to the finish line.

Race Pace

Stride patterns dictate the pace of a 400 metres hurdles race. It is apparent from the study of race statistics that top class hurdlers reach top speed between the first and fifth hurdles and thereafter the athlete who *decelerates the quickest* is the loser.

This premise suggests that there is a relationship between the first and second 200 metres of a 400 metres hurdles race. In the world records set by David Hemery (1968),

TABLE 5

	To the first hurdle	Between hurdles
	19, 20 or 21 strides	13 strides
	21 or 22 strides	14 strides
	22 strides	15 strides
	22 or 23 strides	16 strides
	23 or 24 strides	17 strides

TABLE 6

NAME	RACE PATTERN	TOTAL STRIDES
Novice athlete [male]	23 to H1	
	15's to H5	
	17's to H8	
	19's to H10	
	22 to finish	196
Good club athlete [female]	23 to H1	
	16's to H5	
	17's to H8	
	18's to H10	
	20 to finish	194
Good club athlete [male]	22 to H1	
	15's to H6	
	16's to H10	
	18 to finish	179
Edwin Moses [USA]	19's to H1	
World record 1983 47.06s	13's to H10	
	16 to finish	153
John Akii-Bua [UGA]	21 to H1	
World record 1972 47.82s	13's to H6	
	14's to H9	
	15 to H10	
	16 to finish	159
Dave Hemery [GBR]	21 to H1	
World record 1968 48.1s	13's to H6	
	15's to H10	
	16 to finish	162
Kriss Akabusi [GBR]	20 to H1	
British record 1990 47.92s	13's to H7	
	14's to H9	
	15's to H10	
	16 to finish	158
Sally Gunnell [GBR]	23 to H1	
British record 1988 54.03	15's to H7	
	17's to H10	
	17 to finish	181

Fig. 5

Fig. 6

John Akii-Bua (1972) and Edwin Moses (1983), the differential between their first and second 200 metres was 1.5 seconds, 1.8 seconds and 1.6 seconds respectively. In all top class performances in men's races analysed since 1968, this differential has never been less than 0.6 seconds and never more then 3.0 seconds. In women's races since 1974, the lowest differential has been 1.1 seconds and the highest 4.0 seconds.

Table 7 gives coaches and athletes an indication of touchdown times for athletes at various performance levels. Thus, in training, if an athlete has a touchdown time of 23.3 seconds at the 5th hurdle, then an overall time of approximately 52.0 seconds is indicated, but only if the athlete has a well developed endurance capacity.

Table 8 shows a wide range of performances, from Edwin Moses' world record performance of 1983 to that of a very good club athlete. Similarly, Table 9 shows a range of performances for women.

In analysing such statistics it seems reasonable that the first tactical point for an athlete is to run at a realistically even pace throughout the race. This allows an athlete to use fuel resources in an economical manner. This aspect of 400 metres hurdles is possibly the hardest to learn. A newcomer to the event will probably take 12–18 months to understand this part of the 400 metres hurdler's "trade".

TABLE 7

	48.0	49.0	50.0	52.0	53.0	54.0
Time at Landing after						
1st hurdle	5.9	6.0	6.0	6.1	6.3	6.4
2nd hurdle	9.7	10.0	10.2	10.4	10.7	10.9
3rd hurdle	13.7	14.1	14.4	14.7	15.1	15.4
4th hurdle	17.7	18.2	18.6	19.0	19.5	19.9
5th hurdle	21.7	22.3	22.8	23.3	23.9	24.4
6th hurdle	25.8	26.5	27.1	27.7	28.4	29.0
7th hurdle	29.9	30.8	31.5	32.2	32.9	33.7
8th hurdle	34.2	35.2	36.9	36.8	37.6	38.5
9th hurdle	38.5	39.7	40.4	41.6	42.5	43.4
10th hurdle	43.0	44.3	45.1	46.5	47.5	48.4
Total time	48.0	49.6	50.5	52.0	53.0	54.0

SPLIT TIME CHART—400 METRES HURDLES.
From: "The Hurdle Races" by K. O. Bosen.

Spatial Judgement

This quality is required in many athletic events, but especially in 400 metres hurdles. It can be defined as "the ability to judge space at speed, and to make the necessary corrections without losing speed, balance or control".

Beginners will always seem to arrive either too far away from or too close to a hurdle. This leads to very exaggerated adjustments in the stride pattern when approaching the hurdle. These adjustments cause many problems, the most serious of which are loss of speed and waste of energy. Athletes new to 400 metres hurdling must be made aware of this problem very early in their career. Coaches must ask them to sight a hurdle as early as possible. After leaving a hurdle, look for the next one, sight it, then have a smooth approach to it. It is only by learning this skill that athletes will prevent grossly unequal stride lengths, which in turn cause speed losses and energy wastage.

Starting in 400 Metres Hurdles

Adaptability in all situations is the key word. In sprint hurdling, the athlete usually uses eight strides to the first hurdle, with only small margins for error. In 400 metres hurdles, the athlete has 45 metres from the start to the first hurdle (50 metres for the intermediate women's 300 metres hurdles). As an example, top class hurdlers can take 21 strides from the blocks to hurdle 1. If the hurdler leads with the left leg over hurdle 1, the left foot will be placed in the front block at the start. If there is a very strong head-wind, or the track surface is very poor, then the athlete may have to use an extra stride to get to the first hurdle smoothly and efficiently. This means that the athlete will take 22 strides instead of 21. As a consequence, the athlete must change the feet round in the blocks, with the right foot on the front block.

TABLE 8 (Men)

Athlete	E. Moses (USA) WR 1983			J. Akii-Bua (UGA) WR 1972			D. Hemery (GB) WR 1968			K. Akabusi (GB) GB record			Good Club Athlete		
	1	2	3	1	2	3	1	2	3	1	2	3	1	2	3
To Hurdle 1	5.9	5.9	19	6.1	6.1	21	6.1	6.1	21	6.0	6.0	20	6.2	6.2	22
To Hurdle 2	9.6	3.7	13	9.8	3.7	13	9.8	3.7	13	9.7	3.7	13	10.3	4.1	15
To Hurdle 3	13.4	3.8	13	13.6	3.8	13	13.6	3.8	13	13.6	3.9	13	14.4	4.1	15
To Hurdle 4	17.1	3.7	13	17.4	3.8	13	17.5	3.9	13	17.4	3.8	13	18.7	4.3	15
To Hurdle 5	21.0	3.9	13	21.3	3.9	13	21.5	4.0	13	21.3	3.9	13	23.1	4.4	15
1st 200m time	22.7			23.0			23.3			23.1			25.1		
To Hurdle 6	24.9	3.9	13	25.4	4.1	14	25.4	3.9	13	25.4	4.1	13	27.5	4.4	15
To Hurdle 7	29.0	4.1	13	29.5	4.1	14	29.6	4.2	15	29.5	4.1	13	32.3	4.8	16
To Hurdle 8	33.1	4.1	13	33.7	4.2	14	33.9	4.3	15	33.8	4.3	14	37.2	4.9	16
To Hurdle 9	37.4	4.3	13	38.1	4.4	14	38.3	4.4	15	38.2	4.4	14	42.2	5.0	16
To Hurdle 10	41.9	4.5	13	42.6	4.5	15	42.8	4.5	15	42.7	4.5	15	47.2	5.0	16
H. 10 to Finish	5.12		16	5.2		18	5.3		18	5.22		16	5.7		20
2nd 200m time	24.32			24.8			24.8			24.82			27.8		
Differential	1.62			1.8			1.5			1.72			2.7		
Final Time	47.02			47.82			48.1			47.92			52.9		

Notes: 1 = Touchdown time at each hurdle   2 = Time between each hurdle touchdown   3 = Stride pattern

TABLE 9 (Women)

Athlete	S. Busch (GDR) Rome 1987			T. Ledovskaia (USSR) Seoul 1988			D. Flintoff (AUS) Seoul 1988			S. Gunnell (GB) Seoul 1988			Good Club Athlete		
	1	2	3	1	2	3	1	2	3	1	2	3	1	2	3
To Hurdle 1	6.60	6.60	23	6.36	6.36	23	6.53	6.53	23	6.64	6.64	23	7.1	7.1	24
To Hurdle 2	10.81	4.21	15	10.41	4.05	15	10.69	4.16	15	10.81	4.17	15	11.8	4.7	16
To Hurdle 3	15.19	4.38	15	14.49	4.08	15	14.93	4.24	15	15.09	4.28	15	16.5	4.7	16
To Hurdle 4	19.65	4.46	15	18.69	4.20	15	19.30	4.37	15	19.45	4.36	15	21.5	5.0	16
To Hurdle 5	24.13	4.48	15	23.06	4.37	15	23.71	4.41	15	23.94	4.49	15	26.5	5.0	16
1st 200m time	26.03			24.96			25.61			25.94			28.5		
To Hurdle 6	28.81	4.68	15	27.61	4.55	16	28.26	4.55	15	28.39	4.45	15	31.5	5.0	16
To Hurdle 7	33.59	4.78	15	32.41	4.80	16	32.93	4.67	15	33.11	4.72	15	36.7	5.2	17
To Hurdle 8	38.46	4.87	15	37.27	4.86	16	37.68	4.75	16	38.07	4.96	17	41.9	5.2	17
To Hurdle 9	43.38	4.92	16	42.29	5.02	16	42.64	4.96	16	43.20	5.13	17	47.5	5.6	18
To Hurdle 10	48.31	4.93	16	47.44	5.15	17	47.68	5.04	16	48.28	5.08	17	53.3	5.8	18
H. 10 to Finish	5.31		18	5.74		20	5.49		20	5.75		20	6.7		23
2nd 200m time	27.59			28.23			27.56			28.09			31.5		
Differential	1.56			3.27			1.95			2.15			3.0		
Final Time	53.62			53.18			53.17			54.03			60.0		

Notes: 1 = Touchdown time at each hurdle   2 = Time between each hurdle touchdown   3 = Stride pattern

21

Thus athletes must be well practised in leaving their blocks with either foot forward. It is better to change feet in the blocks when required, rather than taking the first hurdle with the "wrong leg", which disrupts a planned stride pattern.

The start—(begin with the advocate "medium" start)—the approach to the first hurdle and the clearance of the first hurdle set the tone of the race. It is vitally important that athletes are well practised in all the available alternatives.

Tony Jarrett (G.B.), bronze medallist in the 110m Hurdles at the 1991 World Championships in Tokyo. (Photograph by Mark Shearman)

4 Teaching Hurdling

Do not look at the rule book for spacings and heights of hurdles when the teaching process begins. In teaching any technique, the rule is that the event must first be made to suit the participant. In hurdling, the teacher and the coach must use very low hurdles to begin with. The spacing between each hurdle should match the learner's natural stride length. In the last chapter, we learned that hurdling is always a compromise. With beginners we must make the compromise work in their favour, so that they can learn quickly and thus enjoy hurdling. If we resort to the competition handbook for the heights and spacings, the physical dimensions of the situation will be too great for learning to happen. Be prepared to lower the heights of hurdles and shorten the distance between them. Then beginners will know the joy of hurdling.

The best method of organising the compromise in favour of each learner in a group is to use a hurdling grid, as shown in diagram 4. Five flights are set out at varying distances apart. For example, lane "A" can be set out at nine walking strides [of the teacher] apart, and so on, down to lane "E" set out at five walking strides apart. Hurdles can be set at various heights to suit the learners. A common start line can be used, but alternative start lines can be marked to suit an individual's stride pattern to the first hurdle.

The first principle is to establish the pattern of three fast strides between each hurdle. This can start in the gym or the sports hall. Use low benches, skittles and canes or the very small teaching hurdles manufactured nowadays. Use any of this apparatus to encourage the three stride pattern between hurdles. Do not bother about proper hurdle clearance at this stage, but do concentrate on a fast, uninterrupted rhythm, the essence of good hurdling.

SAFETY POINTS WHEN TEACHING

1 Do not allow pupils to clear the hurdles the "wrong way". Hurdles are designed to topple one way only.
2 Do not hurdle on wet grass or slippery surfaces.
3 If you use gym benches, do not put one on top of the other to simulate hurdle height. They are very solid objects and hurt if you hit them!
4 If you use canes and skittles, do not set them too high. The canes can be caught between the learners' legs, which could trip them over.
5 Do not allow beginners to hurdle in spikes. They will probably trip over.

Once the fast three stride pattern is instituted, then the good points of hurdle clearance can be taught.

HURDLE CLEARANCE TEACHING ACTIVITIES

Walking Over Hurdles

REMEMBER!
—if you cannot do something slowly, you cannot do it quickly.
—concentrate on one point at a time. The brain cannot handle more.

DIAGRAM 4

SUGGESTED LAY OUT FOR CLASS TEACHING
(after Le Masurier)

Hurdles in lanes A-E spaced at progressively smaller distances

First hurdles all on the same line. Longer striding boys
in lane 'A'. Shorter striding boys boys in lane 'E'.
All return to start down right side of hurdles.

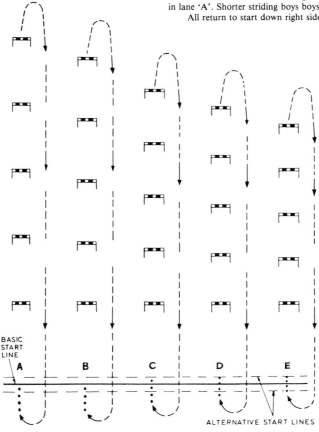

BASIC
START
LINE

A   B   C   D   E

ALTERNATIVE START LINES

Begin with a good demonstration, using video, film, still pictures etc., so that the learners know which the lead leg and the trail leg are. A good visual image to start with will quicken the learning process.

THEN
1 Set up the hurdling grid [Diagram 4].
2 Walk to each hurdle.
   Lift the lead leg up, bent at the knee.
   As the heel of the lead leg reaches hurdle

height, drive the heel forwards.

As the heel passes over the barrier, return the foot to the ground as quickly as possible. [The teacher should observe from head on also, to see if the lead leg is being lifted parallel to the lines on the track.]

3 After the trailing leg leaves the ground, it folds up and is pulled through in a lateral, sweeping action.

4 As the leading foot lands, concentrate on the trailing knee pulling the trailing foot through high and into the next stride.

Having tried the four steps above a number of times, learners who are now confident can continue. As confidence grows, athletes will progress from walking to jogging to running. Five strides between the hurdles for these DRILLS is usually appropriate. As the athletes become more competent and the running and hurdling action speeds up, they should use the three stride pattern. Some learners will take a long time to reach this level of competence, but quick learners can achieve this within one lesson.

At this stage, learners can also be encouraged to "alternate" [see the 400 metres hurdles section], by altering the spaces between hurdles to cause a four stride pattern.

As the running between hurdles and the hurdle clearances improve, begin to emphasise the landing pattern after the hurdle. The lead leg must return to the ground quickly, with the trail leg landing as soon as possible thereafter.

The landing after the hurdle is very important because it allows the hurdler to return to sprinting quickly. This may seem an advanced point for learners, but once learned it will transform a hurdler. On a three stride pattern, ask athletes to listen to their footfalls. The landing sounds like two quick strides, followed by two longer ones:

TA—TA—TAA—TAA

On a five stride drill pattern, it sounds like:

TA—TA—TAA—TAA—TAA—TAA

Emphasise the staccato rhythm of the TA—TA landings.

Fig. 8

Bethan Edwards—young athletes must be aggressive when running off the hurdles.

As outlined at the beginning of this chapter, it is wise when teaching technique to concentrate upon one point at a time. In hurdling we can use "isolation drills" to improve lead leg, trail leg and arm actions separately.

No mention has been made so far of teaching arm action. Usually arms work as opposites to the legs, and it is at this stage that more attention can be given to proper arm action.

You will have noticed that the hurdles set out in the hurdling grid [Diagram 4] have spaces between the rows. This allows athletes to run between the rows and down the side of the hurdles, enabling them to concentrate on the action of the lead leg and the trail leg separately [see figures 9 and 10]. Rhythm, correct landing emphasis and actions of the body parts must be stressed during isolation drills.

TEACHING 300 METRES AND 400 METRES HURDLING

In recent years, the number of hurdling events has increased. Youths and Juniors have 400 metres hurdles events, Intermediate women can now do the 300 metres hurdles, and Junior women can do the 400 metres hurdles. Senior women can contest 400 metres hurdles right through to Olympic level.

Aspiring 400 metres hurdlers should have a sound grounding in sprint hurdling. The virtues of "alternating" have already been emphasised. The early teaching process should include work on "alternating", so that athletes are adept at using either leg as the leading leg.

The ability to alternate allows an athlete to use both an odd number and an even number

Fig. 9

of strides between hurdles during a race. An athlete needs to do this because the fatigue factor is high during a 400 metres hurdle race. As the athlete proceeds, fatigue sets in, particularly after the fifth hurdle. As the athlete fatigues, he will change down and put in a greater number of strides between hurdles. If the athlete can change down from 15 strides to 16 strides, because he can alternate, it will be a much smoother transition than changing from 15 to 17 strides. Athletes must be encouraged to run boldly between and at the hurdles. Novices, especially novice women, will use three strides where two will do. They "back off" as they approach a hurdle and slip in an extra stride. This causes the athlete to slow and it also uses much more energy.

Here are some activities which will help the novice 300 and 400 metre hurdler develop necessary attributes.

HURDLING SKILL

1 To encourage and improve "alternating"
   —run over 5 hurdles placed 4 or 6 running strides apart.
   —run over 5 hurdles placed 10 or 12 running strides apart.
   —normal sprint isolation drills, with the hurdles placed at an even number of strides apart.
2 For the following, hurdles should be placed at the normal 35 metres apart.
   —run from the start to the first hurdle. If the athlete reaches hurdle 1 on the "wrong" foot, try again after changing the feet around in the blocks.
   —run from the start to hurdle 5
   —run from the start to hurdle 8
   —run from the start to hurdle 10

Fig. 10

In the last three activities, rehearsal of a racing pattern is the aim. Substantial fatigue will result, in which case the young athlete must have a full rest recovery before attempting subsequent repetitions.

HURDLING FITNESS

Top class 400 metres hurdlers undertake very arduous training regimes which involve a lot of distressing fatigue running and hurdling. This type of activity is UNSUITABLE for young athletes. There is nothing wrong with young athletes being fatigued. However, complete rest recovery must be allowed before subsequent repetitions.

Activities

Circuit training

Steady running, cross country and fartlek, interval running and continuous relays in the preparation periods.

Fast running and hurdling during the competition periods with repetitions over 40, 80, 150 and 200 metres.

Example schedules are shown in Appendix 1.

ATHLETICS COACH

The Coaching Journal of the B.A.F.

Published:
March, June, September, December

Details from:
Malcolm Arnold
56 Rolls Avenue
Penpedairheol
Hengoed, Mid Glam. CF8 8HQ

5   Training for Hurdling

Hurdlers have many basic fitness require-ments, depending upon their age and stage of development. "Fitness" for any task is a very specific objective. The most basic requirements for hurdlers are:

A high sprinting speed between hurdles.

Limb speed into, over and off the hurdle.

Specific endurance for a particular event.

Good joint mobility in the legs, hips and lower back.

There are further specific requirements which will be discussed later in this chapter.

It should be understood that this chapter contains basic information which the coach and athlete should interpret and use according to their needs. NO athlete has the same ability, aims and objectives as other athletes. It is the skilful interpretation, by the coach, of training rules, methods and activities into meaningful training schedules that is important.

Whether the coach works with novice athletes twice a week or an International training twelve times a week, he has the problem of information assimilation. The transformation of this information into meaningful schedules is most important.

THE TRAINING SESSION

Training sessions should follow a simple, logical pattern. The first function of a coach at the session is to ensure punctuality. Athletes should also be properly dressed for the session.

Thereafter, the session should follow this pattern:

1   WARM UP
Jog 2-4 laps to generate warmth.

2   MOBILITY EXERCISES
In this section do exercises for the neck, the shoulders, the trunk and lower back and the legs and ankles. These activities need not be particularly specific to hurdling. [See the BAAB book "Mobility Training" for examples].

3   SPECIFIC HURDLING MOBILITY EXERCISES
Figures 11 to 25 show Colin Jackson and Kay Morley doing specific hurdling exercises.

4   TECHNICAL WORK

5   FITNESS WORK

6   WARM DOWN
Jog 2-4 laps, allowing athletes to settle down, mentally and physically, after training. Here the coach can also evaluate the training and discuss progress.

PLANNING THE TRAINING YEAR

Having examined the structure of one training session, attention must be focussed on the annual training plan.

The planning of training and the day to day application of plans is regarded as a science in itself. Athletes who are serious, regardless of their standard of performance, deserve to have a proper training plan, so that they can reach a peak of performance at the right time of the year. This type of planning is called PERIODISATION, which simply means breaking down the athlete's year into periods of preparation and competition time.

Fig. 11

Fig. 12

Fig. 13

Fig. 14

31

Fig. 15

Fig. 16

Fig. 17

Fig. 18

Fig. 19

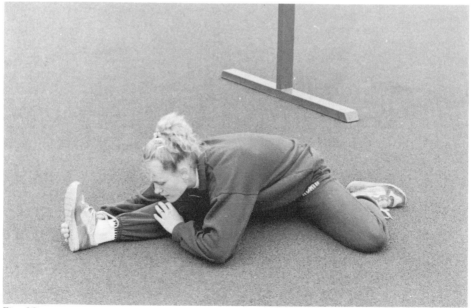

Fig. 20

Fig. 21

Fig. 22

Fig. 23

Fig. 24A

Fig. 24B

Fig. 24C

Fig. 25A

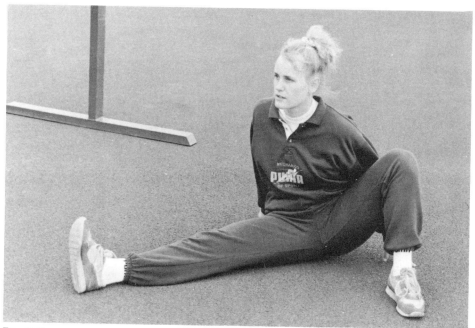

Fig. 25B

The training year is usually broken up into

PREPARATION and COMPETITION

This is followed by the

TRANSITION

which is the time between the end of the competition season and the beginning of the next preparation season.

The theory of periodisation is now well established and is used by the world's leading coaches and athletes. It is possible to have SINGLE PERIODISED YEARS [i.e. one main competitive peak] or DOUBLE PERIODISED YEARS [i.e. two or more main competitive peaks—for example one peak for the indoor season and one for the outdoor season].

Periodisation is a systematic and progressive approach to an athlete's preparation and is recommended.

For school athletes who play other sports, it is also possible to divide their time [say, three or four months of the spring and summer terms] into periods of preparation and competition, taking into account the training they will have done for their other sports.

In general terms, periodisation can be likened to the building of a house. Training is like building a solid foundation upon which the walls and finally the roof can be placed. Without strong foundations and strong walls the roof will eventually collapse. In athletics terms, the foundations of fitness are built in preparation periods out of season. The benefits of that work are then seen in the competitive season.

It is very important that the appropriate work is given to the athlete during each training period. Heavy plodding repetitions are best done in the early preparation time, whilst quick, light, fast work is ideal for producing good competition performances.

In preparation periods the volume of work is high, yet the intensity low. Then there is a systematic transition to the competitive period, where the volume of work is lower and the intensity higher.

Young athletes must not be treated as scaled down adults. They each have their own special needs and features and their training should reflect this.

Training schedules should demand that athletes move from the general to the specific, from preparation periods through to competition periods.

ENERGY PROVISION MECHANISMS

There are numerous energy pathways, some of which are more relevant to hurdlers than others. Extensive physiological texts have been written on this subject. The coach requiring further advanced knowledge should consult sports physiologists. Energy sources can and will be improved by relevant training activities.

Adenosine triphosphate [ATP] is the immediate, usable form of chemical energy available for muscular activity. It is stored in muscle cells. This store is minute. When ATP is used to release energy, it must be rebuilt [resynthesised]. ATP can be resynthesised through various physiological mechanisms, depending upon how the energy is required [e.g. for jogging, sprinting, hurdling, throwing etc.]

The following description will allow coaches a basic understanding of these mechanisms.

Food energy is used to manufacture ATP. For continuous exercise, ATP must be rebuilt at the same rate at which it is used by the body.

Where does ATP come from?

1   It is stored in the muscle cells in minute quantities. This cannot really be called an energy source. It is just a start-up system, which has extremely high power but very low capacity and is used by the hurdler at the start of the race.

2   It can be rebuilt from another substance

stored in the muscles, PHOSPHOCREA-TINE. This is an ANAEROBIC mechanism, just like the use of stored ATP, because it does not require the presence of oxygen to rebuild ATP. This reaction has very high power but low capacity, but is probably sufficient to sustain the energy requirements of the trained sprint hurdler during a race.

3   It is also rebuilt through the breakdown of GLYCOGEN. This process is called GLYCOLYSIS. This is another ANAEROBIC process. Usually, glycogen is always available for resynthesis into ATP. However, the reaction is limited by the build-up in the body of LACTIC ACID, especially when activity is very intense. This reaction still has high power, yet a greater capacity than the phosphocreatine reaction. It is important to both the sprint hurdler and the 400 metre hurdler.

4   It is rebuilt through the OXIDATION OF CARBOHYDRATES and is an AEROBIC process. This reaction has a lower power than the previously mentioned reactions, but a much higher capacity. The reaction is important to all athletes, so that they can maintain the training process. It is important to the 400 metres hurdler in the race situation, because part of the 400 metres hurdles event [up to 20% has been suggested by some authorities] is run aerobically.

5   It is rebuilt through the OXIDATION of FREE FATTY ACIDS. This is another AEROBIC process, but is used solely for low intensity exercise and does not concern the hurdler.

Through this simple explanation, the physiological processes that are important to the hurdler can be identified. Training schedules can be developed to stress these mechanisms and improve energy supplies.

Training schedules should move from the general to the specific, as the year progresses. With that principle in mind, together with the need to stress and develop certain physiological mechanisms, the following training activities are recommended.

RUNNING ENDURANCE

The aim is to develop the heart/lung system and thus good aerobic qualities. Because of the nature of muscle structure, hurdlers [especially sprint hurdlers] might find these activities quite hard to begin with.

ACTIVITIES

DISTANCE RUNNING

Remember that long distance to some athletes is one mile, to others thirty miles or more. Sprint hurdlers, explosive athletes, are likely to be poor distance runners, whilst 400 metres hurdlers must be able to develop good aerobic qualities, with Vo2 maximum values in the same range as the 800 metre runner.

Initially, ask the beginner to run for five minutes, then turn round and run back to the starting point. The distance can be progressively developed during the preparation period into a fifty or sixty minute run for the 400 metre hurdler. Heart rate should be in the 150 beats per minute range during the run. The athlete must aim to run comfortably and without distress. Vary the surfaces used and guard against shin soreness, calf soreness and sore feet.

INTERVAL RUNNING

Follow the principles of the Gerschler/Reindell regime. Mature athletes can start with a session of 10×200 metres in 35 seconds, with 90 seconds recovery between each run. This session can be developed to 2 sets of 10×200 metres as cardio-vascular fitness improves. Adaptation can be enhanced as athletes improve by:

   i   Decreasing the rest between each run

ii Increasing the speed of each run, or

iii Increasing the number of repetitions.

Interval training is very boring, especially to the explosive athlete. Sugar the pill for hurdlers by organising the interval training as continuous relays, in a semi-competitive situation. Monotony deadens the spirit!

FARTLEK RUNNING
This is a Swedish word, meaning "speed-play". The athlete should run for a certain length of time and during the run there should be variation of pace, with long sustained sections, fast bursts, hill runs and even walking sections. The pace varies according to how the athlete feels. The runs should be done in the countryside in an invigorating environment. As the hurdler improves, he should learn to increase the pressure on himself during the run.

SAND HILL RUNNING
Courses, repetitions and sets should be determined by the coach according to local terrain and the fitness and age of the athletes.

"BACK TO BACKS" or "TURNABOUTS"
This can be done with or without hurdles. A typical session for a mature athlete might be 2 sets of 4 repetitions × 80 metres, with a 30 second turn around and 2–5 minutes between sets. For a 400 metre hurdler, hurdles can be placed 6 hurdling strides apart, within the 80 metre distance.

HARNESS RUNNING
The harness should be held by a responsible person, applying an appropriate resistance over distances up to 30 metres. Alternatively, the harness can be attached to an old car tyre, which the athlete can drag over a cinder or grass surface. The load can be altered by placing shot within the rim of the tyre.

DEVELOPING STRENGTH ENDURANCE

Strength endurance is usually defined as "*the capacity to maintain the contractile force of the muscles, in the climate of endurance*"

This quality can be best developed by the following methods:

HILL RUNNING
Ideally, this should be done over distances of 150–200 metres, up a gradual incline of 15 degrees. Local circumstances often dictate otherwise.

Four repetitions in sets of 1–4 should be attempted, according to the condition of the athlete. There should be a walk back recovery between repetitions and 2–5 minutes rests between sets.

DEVELOPING SPEED ENDURANCE

This is usually defined as "*running very fast in the climate of endurance*"

This quality can be developed by using some of the following methods.

"FLAT OUT RUNS", at 10%-20% more than race distance.

Distances and repetitions	
Sprint hurdlers	120 metres × 6
	150 metres × 6
	200 metres × 3
400 metres hurdlers	250 metres × 3
	300 metres × 3
	440 metres × 2
	50 second run × 2

Rhythm for these runs is a level, very fast pace. The athletes must feel loose, light and relaxed. They can become physically distressed towards the end of the session.

There should be complete rest recovery between repetitions, usually never less than 15 minutes and up to 30 minutes between the longer repetitions.

"BROKEN RUNNING"

Distances up to 150 metres can be run, with the rhythm during the run of:
"Accelerate to top speed"
"Decelerate to approximately 90% of top speed"
"Accelerate again and hold top speed".

Thus, over a 150 metres run, the actual pattern would be:-
Accelerate to, and hold top speed for 60 metres.
Decelerate for 30 metres.
Accelerate to top speed again, and hold for the final 60 metres.

Any distance up to 150 metres can be broken down into this pattern, with 6-8 repetitions in 1 or 2 sets, with 2-3 minutes between repetitions.

ABSOLUTE SPEED

Absolute running speed is fundamental to fast hurdling. An athlete's innate ability is a very strong determining factor, but an athlete's ability to run faster can be developed and improved.

Sprint hurdlers must aim to be fast over 60 metres, 100 metres and 200 metres. 300 and 400 metre hurdlers must aim to be fast over 200 metres, 300 metres, 400 metres and 600 metres.

This type of running should be done to develop maximal speed when building to a peak in competition periods. These sessions can also be used as speed retention sessions during preparation periods.

TEMPO RUNNING

[Suitable for all athletes, young and old]

The distance is split into thirds. Build speed for the first third, develop it further in the next third, then run maximally for the final third. The athletes should feel quick, light and loose during the run. Leg speed must be maintained.

Athletes must keep a quick striding rate in the fastest part of the run. DO NOT OVER-STRIDE when running quickly.

Distances   90 metres [30/30/30]
             120 metres [40/40/40]
             150 metres [50/50/50]

ACCELERATION RUNNING

[Suitable for all athletes]

The rhythm for each run is:
—build towards top speed for 20 metres
—run very fast [high leg speed] in the central portion
—slow down during the last 20 metres.

There should be one set of six or two sets of four repetitions, with a complete rest recovery between reps.

Distances   60 metres [20/20/20]
             90 metres [20/50/20]
             120 metres [20/80/20]

RACE ANALYSIS

Analysis of race patterns gives an important indication of the types of activity which should be done in training.

SPRINT HURDLING

Up to 40 metres	[Start to H4]	— acceleration
40-90 metres	[H4-H8]	— maintain top speed
90 metres-Finish	[H9 and H10]	— hold form and leg speed

300 and 400 METRES HURDLING

Up to H2	—accelerate to top speed
H2 to H8	—hold optimum speed
H8 to Finish	—hold as much form and speed as fatigue allows

TRAINING SESSIONS USED TO DEVELOP VARIOUS ASPECTS OF THE RACE

From the preceding race analysis, it is a straightforward task to set sessions for hurdlers, depending on the time of the year.

SPRINT HURDLES

EXAMPLE SESSIONS

Acceleration [full rest recovery between repetitions]
2×2 hurdles, to set blocks and familiarise for all sessions, then—
1   1×6 hurdles $+ 4 \times 4$ hurdles OR
2   6×4 hurdles OR
3   4×4 hurdles $+ 2 \times 2$ hurdles

Acceleration and top speed maintenance sessions
2×2 hurdles, to set blocks and familiarise, then—
1   1×8 hurdles $+ 2 \times 6$ hurdles
     $+ 2 \times 4$ hurdles OR
2   2×8 hurdles $+ 3 \times 6$ hurdles

Endurance sessions
2×2 hurdles, to set blocks and familiarise, then—
1   1×12 hurdles $+ 2 \times 10$ hurdles
     $+ 1 \times 8$ hurdles OR
2   2×12 hurdles $+ 2 \times 10$ hurdles OR
3   4×12 hurdles

This endurance sprint hurdling is vital for successful competition endurance. On occasions, because of the weather or fatigue, the hurdles should be brought closer together by 1 or even 2 foot lengths to cause better leg speed.

400 METRES HURDLES

400 metres hurdlers, like sprint hurdlers, "learn their trade" over a long period of time.

Most of the world's great 400 metre hurdlers have also been good sprint hurdlers, so hurdling is second nature to them. Young athletes should practise alternating from the start of their careers. Some of the following practices will help in developing race patterns.

1   ALTERNATING
—run over 5 hurdles spaced 6 or 8 running strides apart.
—Isolation drills and full drills, over barriers spaced 4 strides apart.
—Runs over hurdles at normal race distance of 35 metres.

2   ADJUSTMENT FOR LANE DRAW
—Athletes should practise starting from every lane. As one moves from lane 8 to lane 1, the bend tightens considerably and causes different problems.

3   RACE PACE
—Target times must be worked out for various sections of the race and practised.
—practices to rehearse the race pace are set out as follows:

Acceleration
2×2 hurdles for block settings and familiarisation then—
4×3 hurdles very fast, long rest recovery. OR
1×4 hurdles $+ 2 \times 3$ hurdles

Acceleration and speed maintenance
2×2 hurdles set up then—
1×8 hurdles $+ 1 \times 6$ hurdles $+ 2 \times 5$ hurdles OR
1×8 hurdles $+ 1 \times 7$ hurdles $+ 1 \times 6$ hurdles $+ 1 \times 5$ hurdles

Race rehearsal
2×2 hurdles set up then—
2×10 hurdles with 30 minutes between repetitions OR
1×10 hurdles $+ 2 \times 8$ hurdles, full rest recovery between repetitions.

DEVELOPING HURDLING SKILL THROUGH DRILLS

Many drills have been developed with the aim of improving hurdling skill. Young athletes and their coaches sometimes mimic these drills and very often they are done aimlessly, badly and for the wrong reasons. Hurdling drills should be done for the following reasons:

—to isolate limbs to improve their path over the hurdle

—to isolate limbs to improve their speed over the hurdle

—to examine take-off and landing patterns and rhythms

—to improve limb control

Never do drills aimlessly! Do them for a particular purpose and make sure that aim is achieved.

General points on sprint hurdles drills:

1 Drills can be done with hurdles spaced 1, 3 or 5 strides apart.

2 Ensure that the hurdles are spaced at proper distances so that technique is not compromised. As an example of bad practice, a seven stride pattern between hurdles, spaced at competition distances, will put the athlete too close to the hurdle at take-off. Thus the athlete will practise bad technique. The remedy is to stretch the distance between each of the hurdles by four foot lengths and run 5 strides between hurdles, not 7. If the distance is still not right, it can be adjusted for subsequent runs.

3 Hurdle clearances, and the run between hurdles, should be smooth and rhythmic. Never run with shortened, unnatural strides.

Fig. 26   *Colin Jackson. 1 Stride between isolation drills. Hurdles at 3 feet high.*

4 When using isolation drills, know what the pattern of movement should be. Emphasise the speed of the isolated leg, but also emphasise the speed of the other leg. Observe top class hurdlers when they do their drills.

5 After doing isolation drills, always return to and practise the full hurdling action.

Some drills which are useful are: Lead leg isolation over 5 hurdles, with 1, 3 or 5 strides between. [Never use 7 strides].

Trail leg isolation, as above.

Full action, with 3 or 5 strides between.

For all these drills, coach and athlete must work out the distances required between hurdles. Always run smoothly between hurdles, with the correct stride length. Emphasise the fast TA-TA rhythm on landing

DEVELOPING STRENGTH

The body is an incredibly adaptive mechanism, and specific types of strength acquisition can be pursued depending on the requirement of the athlete and on how the muscles are loaded.

The broad categories of strength types are:

ENDURANCE STRENGTH

A basic requirement for hurdlers. It is developed at the beginning of the training year and maintained throughout competition periods.

This type of strength is acquired through circuit training, stage training and lifting low weights at high repetitions, and is suitable for all categories of athlete.

ELASTIC or REBOUND STRENGTH

Another basic requirement for hurdlers. It is acquired during early training phases and developed to a high degree during competition phases.

This type of strength is acquired through hopping and bounding activities, depth jumping, weight lifting with bar and disc, and combinations of jumping and lifting. It is suitable for most categories of athlete, except the very young where jumping activities alone are considered suitable.

GROSS or MAXIMUM STRENGTH

This is also a basic requirement for the adult hurdler. It is acquired exclusively through lifting very heavy weights, which is why it is suitable for physically mature adults only.

Having identified the types of strength, it is necessary to examine the methods of developing them.

The following terminology should first be understood:

1 REPETITION MAXIMUM

All lifting should be done with reference to this point. It is the heaviest weight an athlete can lift in 1 repetition. With physically immature athletes and with adults whose technique is not yet fully developed, 1 repetition maximum must be ESTIMATED by the coach. To do otherwise, by actually attempting to lift 100% maximum, would be dangerous and foolish.

PERCENTAGE OF 1 REPETITION MAXIMUM

Weights lifted by an athlete should be worked out exactly. The weight is calculated as a percentage of his 1 repetition maximum.

REPETITIONS

Repetitions relate to the number of times a bar is lifted in 1 set.

SETS

Sets determine the total number of repetitions of one exercise during a training session.

The relationship between repetitions, sets and percentages of maximum are set out in the following Table 10. [from "Fundamentals of Sports Training"—Matveyev—1977].

Strength acquisition should take account of the following principles:

TABLE 10

Relative Intensity	% of maximum	No. of reps per set
Maximum	100	1
Sub-maximum	99–90	2–3
High 1	89–80	4–6
High 2	79–70	7–10
Moderate 1	69–60	11–15
Moderate 2	59–50	16–20
Low 1	49–40	21–30
Low 2	39–30	31+

PROGRESSIVE OVERLOAD

Muscles must be overloaded [i.e. worked very hard] if they are to become stronger. This must be done progressively over a long period. There are no short cuts. Attempts to produce quick strength gains usually cause stress injuries. Weight lifting can become very competitive during training, but athletes must only lift the weight related to their strength and technical ability.

SPECIFICITY

Hurdlers must choose lifts and regimes specific to hurdling. The correct schedule must be designed for them.

REVERSIBILITY

In the short term, if the athlete stops weight training its beneficial effects will be lost. It is common to reduce the *volume* of loadings during peak competition periods.

ACQUISITION AND RETENTION OF STRENGTH

As a general rule, fitness for any objective is difficult to achieve, yet easier to maintain. The most difficult task in a strength training regime is the acquisition phase. Strength subsides at a slower rate than it develops. It is suggested that 1 lifting session per week is sufficient to maintain strength levels, providing maximum contractions are used. Personal experience indicates that women lose their strength levels more quickly than men and the training schedule should be adjusted accordingly.

The following training activities are offered as examples of strength training, within the periodised year.

CIRCUIT TRAINING
[two or three times per week].

Stage I

Choose eight exercises and carry them out in this order. Star jumps, Squat thrusts, Cross sit-ups, Back raises on a bench, Bench jumps, Press-ups, Side raises on a bench, Trail leg circling.

Do one exercise for 20 seconds, followed by a 40 second rest.

Do three circuits, having 2 minutes rest between each circuit.

Stage II

As athletes adapt to the overload, increase the work periods and decrease the rest intervals.

Do the same exercises for 30 seconds, followed by a 30 second rest, having 1 or 1½ minutes rest between circuits.

Stage III

Continue to increase the work load at the pace of the athletes. Do the same exercises for 30 seconds on, 30 seconds off, but increase to 4 circuits, with 1 or 1½ minutes rest between. This third stage coincides with the final phase of pre-competition training. At times of competition, circuits should be done at least once per week.

Of course, there are many ways of setting up circuit training and coaches are urged to use their imagination. Suggestions are just a beginning and modifications can be made to develop these ideas, according to circumstance and situation.

HOPPING AND BOUNDING

Experiences during recent years have led me to believe that hopping and bounding causes ankle, shin and knee injury if not administered correctly. Also, I believe that lifting with bar and disc causes quicker and more valuable strength gains for the sprinter and hurdler.

I still believe that bounding sessions are valuable as long as the leg stresses are carefully monitored. It is a very good activity for young athletes.

Bearing in mind these warnings, hopping and bounding should be introduced and progressed as follows.

TEACH THE TECHNIQUE
1 Foot contact with the ground is not a pounding action, but a reaching and pawing one, done on a flat foot. Watch the good triple jumper for a demonstration of this action.
2 The trunk and head should be upright during jumping.
3 The hips should be under the trunk—do not let the bottom stick out.
4 Arms should swing alternately, vigorously and in harmony with the legs.
   Develop the teaching and practise jumping by using individual jumps such as:
   Standing long jump
   Standing triple jump
   2 hops, 2 steps and a jump

5 bunny jumps
Running 4 hops and a jump
Timed 25 metre hop
A Jumps Decathlon table is available for use which adds variety and interest. This table can be found in the BAF Long Jump and Triple Jump books and in the publication "But First ...."

Once the technique has been learned, suggested sessions are:

WINTER REGIME [2 per week]
Choose 3 exercises, say,

Hopping on the right leg
Hopping on the left leg and
Hop-hop-step-step rhythm

Start with 2 sets of 12 ground contacts for each exercise, then increase the overload as the athlete adapts.

SUMMER REGIME [1 per week, as far away from competition as possible]
Use the same exercises, but use six ground contacts, doing them in a lighter, quicker fashion.

Other activities can be used, such as jumping up and down stadium steps, jumping from gymnasium boxes and combination jumping over hurdles. Coaches should seek to use their natural surroundings for this type of work, but remember the warning about leg damage through overuse on these activities.

LIFTING WITH BAR AND DISC

This activity is a very sensible method of gaining all types of strength by hurdlers. Young athletes can lift using bar and disc, as long as technique is learned properly first with adequate expert supervision, and as long as the weight on the bar is suitable to their stage of development.

The following regime is an example of the type of lifting I have used with top class sprinters and hurdlers in recent years.

STAGE I
Develop basic strength and good lifting technique, using simple sets of 6 × 75% maximum for each lift. The principle lifts used for leg and trunk development are the half squat [knees to 90 degrees on full bend], the power clean, the snatch and the bench press, supplemented by numerous upper body and stomach exercises.

STAGE II
Develop maximum strength through various "pyramids".

STAGE III
Further develop maximum strength through "pyramids" and combined methods.

COMPETITION PERIODS
To maintain strength acquired in preparation periods.

The following is a diagrammatic representation of a lifting regime used during a periodised year:

During the hectic competition season it is sometimes difficult to keep a normal frequency of lifting. The athlete should aim to lift to somewhere near maximum at least every 7–10 days.

1 repetition maximums [in kilograms] for each lift are shown opposite for some currently successful hurdlers.

Other lifts used include bent-over rowing and variations on the seated press.

DEVELOPING MOBILITY

Mobility development is the daily bread of the hurdler. A day should not go by without at least 30 minutes mobility work. Within a training session, general mobility exercises must be followed by specific hurdling exercises. A number of these exercises are demonstrated by current Commonwealth champions Colin Jackson and Kay Morley in figures 11 to 25.

Most of the specific hurdling exercises are for the lower back, hips and hamstring areas. Exercises should be of the slow stretching type. The following regime is suggested:
1   Identify the exercise.

PHASE	SETS	REPS.	%MAX.	FREQUENCY
I	3	8	75	3/week
II	1	5,4,3,2,1	80–100	3/week
III	half squat 3 combined with rebound jumps 3 then power cleans 3 and half squats, power clean, bench press 1	6 12 6 1,3,2,1,1,1	80 80 90–95–100–97–95	1/week 1/week

ATHLETE	Half Squat	Power clean	Snatch	Bench Press
C. Jackson	240	137.5	92.5	120
N. Walker	250	125	80	120
P. Gray	205	115	77.5	117.5
K. Morley	160	80	52.5	60

Fig. 27

Colin Jackson performing a Half Squat with a heavy bar. Inexperienced lifters must have a person at each end of the bar, as a safety measure.

2 Reach the "end" position for the exercise—that point where the muscle begins to reach full stretch.
3 Hold that point for up to 15 seconds.
4 Relax for up to 10 seconds.
5 Do at least 8 repetitions of each exercise.

The BAF book "Mobility Training" examines this topic in great detail, and will be a useful purchase for the hurdler and the coach.

THE COMPLETE TRAINING PROCESS

The whole process of training can be logically thought out, for both the beginner and the expert. Individuals have their strengths and weaknesses, depending upon age and stage of development. The following summary will provide a template for planning the programme:

1 Identify the competition period.
2 Identify the most important competitions during that period.
3 Divide the year into
PREPARATION
COMPETITION
TRANSITION
4 Identify the aspects of fitness required during a particular training period.
5 Identify the methods required to produce that fitness.
6 Estimate the time the athlete has for training.
7 Plan a scheme of work.

Fig. 28

Nigel Walker performing a Power Clean.

Appendix 1

EXAMPLES OF TRAINING SCHEDULES

These schedules are not meant to be definitive, because coaches and athletes work in a particular situation, fulfilling their own needs. They are suggested starting points. Discussions with established athletes and experienced coaches are recommended.

SPRINT HURDLES

COMPLETE BEGINNERS

1 Jog two laps of the track.
2 Mobility exercises.
3 Using hurdles grid, establish the pattern of eight strides to hurdle one and three strides between hurdles.
4 Hurdle walking, establishing the lead and trail leg movement patterns.
5 Amalgamate activities 3 and 4 for good hurdling over low barriers.
6 Warm down.

YOUNG CLUB ATHLETES

A Training twice per week in Winter

Session One
1 Warm up by jogging.
2 Mobility exercises.
3 Isolated lead and trail leg skills at 5 strides between × 4, followed by 3 strides × 4.
4 Full hurdling action at 5 between × 4 and 3 between × 4, from a standing start.
5 Continuous relay.
6 Warm down.

Session Two
1 Warm up by jogging.
2 Mobility exercises.
3 Isolated lead and trail leg exercises, followed by the full action.
4 4 × 10 hurdles at three strides between, with a full recovery. Bring the hurdles closer if necessary.
5 4 acceleration runs over 60 metres. Full rest recovery.
6 Warm down.

B Training twice per week in Summer

Session One
1 Warm up by jogging.
2 Mobility exercises.
3 Hurdles skill drills.
4 4 × 3 hurdles from blocks.
   2 runs over full distance (10 mins rest between).
5 Rest.
6 4 × 60 metres acceleration run, building up for 20 metres, sprinting hard for 20 metres, then slowing down for 20 metres. Walk back recovery.
7 Warm down.

Session Two
1 Warm up by jogging.
2 Mobility exercises.
3 Hurdles skill drills.
4 2 × 4 hurdles from blocks.
   2 × 8 hurdles from blocks.
   1 × 10 hurdles from blocks.
5 Rest.
6 4 × 80 metres sprinting. Full recovery between runs.
7 Warm down.

MATURE CLUB ATHLETES

A   Training four times per week in Winter

B   Training four times per week in Summer

Session One
1   Warm up.
2   Mobility exercises and skill drills.
3   Circuit (with weights).
4   Aerobic run at a relaxed pace.
5   Warm down.

Session Two
1   Warm up.
2   Mobility exercises.
3   Skill drills—isolated and complete aspects.
4   4×8 hurdles (at a reduced height) for rhythm.
    Easy walk back recovery.
5   Rest.
6   6×8 hurdles (at normal height) for rhythm, speed and improvement of technique. Easy walk-back recovery.
7   Warm down.
    (N.B. Reduce distances between hurdles where necessary).

Session Three
1   Warm up.
2   Mobility exercises.
3   Sprint drills.
4   Run 200 metres, jog/walk 100 metres $\times 6$ to 10 repetitions.
5   Warm down.

Session Four
1   Warm up.
2   Mobility exercises.
3   Hurdles skill practices.
4   $1 \times 6H, 1 \times 8H, 1 \times 10H, 1 \times 11H, 1 \times 12H$.
    (Reduce hurdles distances where necessary).
5   Rest.
6   Circuit.
7   Warm down.

Session One
1   Warm up.
2   Mobility exercises.
3   Hurdles skill practices.
4   1×2 hurdles from blocks.
    6×4 hurdles from blocks.
5   4×90 metres high speed runs. Long rest recovery.
6   Warm down.

Session Two
1   Warm up.
2   Mobility exercises.
3   Hurdles skill practices.
4   3×8 hurdles.
5   $6 \times$ acceleration runs (20 metres–20 metres–20 metres).
6   Warm down.

Session Three
1   Warm up.
2   Mobility exercises.
3   Hurdles skill practices.
4   4×10 hurdles—complete rest recovery.
5   Speed endurance activity.
6   Warm down.

Session Four
1   Warm up.
2   Mobility exercises.
3   Sprint drills.
4   Acceleration runs over 60 metres $\times 4$.
5   $2 \times 4 \times 150$ metres. Walk between repetitions, 15 minutes between sets.
6   Warm down.

400 METRES HURDLES

COMPLETE BEGINNERS
A similar session to that for sprint hurdles is suggested. Work should also be included which requires the athlete to "alternate" the leading leg, such as:

a)   4 × 6 hurdles, with 4 strides between.
b)   4 × 6 hurdles, with 6 strides between.

YOUNG CLUB ATHLETES

A   Training twice per week in Winter

Session One
1   Warm up by jogging.
2   Mobility exercises.
3   Isolated lead and trail leg skills followed by full action with 4 or 6 strides between hurdles, so that athletes must alternate.
4   4 × 5 hurdles at full 400 hurdles distance, practising the stride pattern and the rhythm of running.
5   Warm down.

Session Two
1   Warm up by jogging.
2   Mobility exercises.
3   Isolated lead and trail leg skills, followed by full action, at 5 strides between. First the "good" legs must be used, followed by the "wrong" legs.
4   4 × 3 hurdles at full 400 hurdles distance.
5   Continuous relay.
6   Warm down.

B   Training twice per week in Summer

Session One
1   Warm up by jogging.
2   Mobility exercises.
3   Isolated skills and full action skills as session one in the Winter.
4   1 × 5 hurdles, 1 × 8 hurdles and 1 × 10 hurdles. Long rest recovery.

5   Relaxed running over 60 metres × 4 at 85% maximum speed. Long rest recovery.
6   Warm down.

Session Two
1   Warm up by jogging.
2   Mobility exercises.
3   Hurdles skill drills.
4   2 × 2 hurdles—2 × 5 hurdles with long rest recovery.
5   4 × 150 metres, with a long rest recovery.
6   Warm down.

MATURE CLUB ATHLETES

A   Training four times per week in Winter

Session One
1   Warm up by jogging.
2   Mobility exercises.
3   Hurdles skills, practising isolated drills, alternating and full action.
4   Steady 20 minutes running, increasing to 40 minutes over 12 weeks. Running should be on grass and can be in the form of "fartlek".
5   Warm down.

Session Two
1   Warm up by jogging.
2   Mobility exercises.
3   Hurdles drills.
4   3 × 8 hurdles. Develop stride patterns, if weather allows. Good rest recovery.
5   Circuit training.

Session Three
1   Warm up by jogging.
2   Mobility exercises.
3   Sprint drills.
4   1 × 10 × 200 metres. Each 200 metres should be done in approximately 35 seconds, with a 90 second walk/jog between each 200. Over 12 weeks, progress to 2 × 8 × 200 metres in 32

seconds with 60 seconds between each 200 metres.
5 Warm down.

Session Four
1 Warm up by jogging.
2 Mobility exercises.
3 Hurdles turnabouts. 10 hurdles set out at 6 strides apart in two sets of five, one set facing one way, the other set facing the opposite way. 6 × 2 shuttle runs with 60 seconds between each run. Progress over 12 weeks by diminishing the interval to 30 seconds.
4 Circuit training.
5 Warm down.

B Training four times per week in Summer

Session One
1 Warm up by jogging.
2 Hurdles drills, practising alternating.
3 2 × 3 hurdles, 2 × 10 hurdles. Long rest recoveries.
4 4 × acceleration 60 metres at 90% maximum speed. Long rest recovery.
5 Warm down.

Session Two
1 Warm up by jogging.
2 Mobility exercises.
3 Hurdles drills.

4 2 × 2 hurdles, 2 × 3 hurdles, 1 × 6 hurdles. Very fast with long rest recovery.
5 3 × 200 metres, very fast with long rest recovery.

Session Three
1 Warm up by jogging.
2 Mobility exercises.
3 2 × 440 metres (or 2 × 50 second runs) very fast, 20-30 minutes recovery.
4 4 × acceleration 60's at 90% maximum speed
5 Warm down.

Session Four
1 Warm up by jogging.
2 Mobility exercises.
3 6 × 150, fast with walk back recovery.
4 3 × start to hurdle 10, practising the racing stride pattern. Long rest recovery.
5 Warm down.

WARNING

The training sessions illustrated are neither exhaustive nor definitive. They are meant as a guide. Training schedules must be set by coach and athlete in the light of the athlete's ability, state of development, state of fitness and the facilities and time available. Please read this book and then set schedules that are relevant to your athlete in his or her situation.

Appendix 2

PROGRESSIVE PERFORMANCE LISTS
WORLD RECORDS

Marks shown in the FIRST COLUMN represent the official World Records as ratified by the IAAF from its inception in 1913 through to the end of 1992. Any significant difference vis a vis actual performance is indicated in parentheses.

Marks shown in the SECOND COLUMN, although equal to/or better than official records, were never submitted to the IAAF but are believed to be statistically valid by ATFS historians.

110m HURDLES [MEN]

Best pre-IAAF performance

15.2y		A. Kraenzlain	(USA)	Chicago	18.6.98
15.4		A. Kraenzlain	(USA)	Paris	14.7.00
15.2y		G. Smith	(NZL)	Auckland	8.3.02
15.2y		J. Gorrels	(USA)	Evanstown	9.6.06
15.2y		J. Gorrels	(USA)	Cambridge	1.6.07
15.2y		A. Shaw	(USA)	Philadelphia	9.5.08
15.0		F. Smithson	(USA)	London	25.7.08
	14.8y	E. Thomson	(CAN)	Columbia	27.5.16
	14.6y	R. Simpson	(USA)	Columbia	27.5.16
	14.6y	R. Simpson	(USA)	Evanston	3.6.16
14.4y		E. Thomson	(CAN)	Philadelphia	29.5.20
14.8		E. Thomson	(CAN)	Antwerp	18.8.20
	14.4y	E. Thomson	(CAN)	Chicago	18.6.21
	14.5	H. Trossbach	(GER)	Frankfurt	16.8.25
14.8	(14.7)	S. Pattersson	(SWE)	Stockholm	18.9.27
	14.8	H. Leistner	(USA)	Palo Alto	12.5.28
	14.4y	S. Anderson	(USA)	Missoula	2.6.28
	14.6	L. Dye	(USA)	Los Angeles	16.6.28
	14.8h	R. Nichols	(USA)	Cambridge	6.7.28
	14.8	S. Anderson	(USA)	Cambridge	6.7.28
	14.8h	G. W. Smith	(SA)	Amsterdam	31.7.28
	14.8s1	L. Dye	(USA)	Amsterdam	31.7.28
	14.8s2	S. Anderson	(USA)	Amsterdam	31.7.28
14.6s3		G. W. Smith	(SA)	Amsterdam	31.7.28
	14.4y	S. Anderson	(USA)	Eugene	1.6.29
14.4		E. Wennstrom	(SWE)	Stockholm	25.8.29
	14.4	S. Anderson	(USA)	Oslo	31.7.30
	14.3y	J. Keller	(USA)	Columbus	2.5.31

Appendix 2

14.2y		P. Beard	(USA)	Lincoln	4.7.31
14.4		B. Sjostadt	(FIN)	Helsinki	5.9.31
	14.4	G. Saling	(USA)	Iowa City	28.5.32
	14.4	B. Harker	(USA)	El Monte	4.6.32
	14.2 (14.1y)	G. Saling	(USA)	Chicago	11.6.32
14.4		P. Beard	(USA)	Cambridge	18.6.32
14.4s		G. Saling	(USA)	Iowa City	25.6.32
14.4		J. Keller	(USA)	Palo Alto	16.6.32
14.4s		G. Saling	(USA)	Los Angeles	2.8.32
	14.2y	P. Beard	(USA)	San Francisco	14.8.32
	14.2y	A. Moreau	(USA)	Baton Rouge	6.5.33
	14.1y	J. Keller	(USA)	Evanston	20.5.33
	14.2y	A. Meier	(USA)	Chicago	17.6.33
	14.3	J. Morriss	(USA)	Chicago	20.6.33
14.4		J. Morriss	(USA)	Budapest	12.8.33
	14.3	J. Morriss	(USA)	Paris	17.8.33
14.4		J. Morriss	(USA)	Turin	8.9.33
	14.4	P. Beard	(USA)	Milwaukee	30.6.34
14.3		P. Beard	(USA)	Stockholm	26.7.34
14.2		P. Beard	(USA)	Oslo	6.8.34
14.2		A. Moreau	(USA)	Oslo	2.8.35
	14.2	A. Moreau	(USA)	Vienna	17.8.35
	14.1yh	F. Towns	(USA)	Birmingham, Al.	15.5.36
	14.1y	F. Towns	(USA)	Birmingham, Al.	16.5.36
	14.1	F. Towns	(USA)	New Orleans	23.5.36
	14.1y	R. Staley	(USA)	Columbus	13.6.36
14.1h		F. Towns	(USA)	Chicago	19.6.36
14.1s		F. Towns	(USA)	Berlin	6.8.36
13.7		F. Towns	(USA)	Oslo	27.8.36
13.7		F. Wolcott	(USA)	Philadelphia	29.6.41
13.6y		H. Dillard	(USA)	Lawrence	17.4.48
13.5y		D. Attlesey	(USA)	Fresno	13.5.50
13.6		D. Attlesey	(USA)	College Park	24.6.50
13.5		D. Attlesey	(USA)	Helsinki	10.7.50
13.4		J. Davis	(USA)	Bakersfield	22.6.56
	(13.3y)	J. Davis	(USA)	Bendigo	17.11.56
13.2	(13.56)	M. Lauer	(GER)	Zurich	7.7.59
13.2		L. Calhoun	(USA)	Bern	21.8.60
13.2	(13.43)	E. McCullouch	(USA)	Minneapolis	16.7.67
13.2		W. Davenport	(USA)	Zurich	4.7.69
13.0ys		R. Milburn	(USA)	Eugene	25.6.71
13.2	(13.24)	R. Milburn	(USA)	Munich	7.9.72
13.0y		R. Milburn	(USA)	Eugene	20.6.73
13.1	(13.41)	R. Milburn	(USA)	Zurich	6.7.73
13.1		R. Milburn	(USA)	Siena	22.7.73
	13.0y	R. Milburn	(USA)	El Paso	10.5.75
	13.1 (13.28)	G. Drut	(FRA)	St. Etienne	29.6.75
13.1		G. Drut	(FRA)	St. Maur	23.7.75
13.0		G. Drut	(FRA)	Berlin	22.8.75
	12.8	R. Nehemiah	(USA)	Kingston	11.5.79

Automatic Timing (Since May 1977)

13.24	R. Milburn	(USA)	Munich	7.9.72
13.21	A. Casanas	(CUB)	Sofia	21.8.77
13.16	R. Nehemiah	(USA)	San Jose	14.4.79
13.00	R. Nehemiah	(USA)	Westwood	6.5.79
12.93	R. Nehemiah	(USA)	Zurich	19.8.81
12.92	R. Kingdom	(USA)	Zurich	16.8.89

y = made at 120 yards.

400m HURDLES [MEN]

Best pre-IAAF Performance

56.4s		H. Hillman	(USA)	London	21.7.08
55.0		C. Bacon	(USA)	London	22.7.08
	54.6y	W. Meanix	(USA)	Cambridge	16.7.15
	54.8y	W. Hummel	(USA)	Newark	9.9.16
	54.8y	F. Smart	(USA)	St. Louis	1.9.17
	54.2y	J. Watt	(USA)	Philadelphia	30.4.20
54.2y		J. Norton	(USA)	Pasadena	26.6.20
54.0		F. Loomis	(USA)	Antwerp	16.8.20
	53.4y	A. Deach	(USA)	Pasadena	5.7.21
	52.1	I. Riley	(USA)	Ann Arbor	31.5.24
	53.2	C. Coulter	(USA)	Iowa City	31.5.24
	52.6	M. Taylor	(USA)	Cambridge	14.6.24
	52.6	M. Taylor	(USA)	Colombus	7.7.24
	53.8y	M. Taylor	(USA)	San Francisco	4.7.25
53.8		S. Pattersson	(SWE)	Colombus	4.10.25
54.2y		Lord Burghley	(GBR)	London	2.7.27
54.6y		J. Gibson	(USA)	Lincoln	2.7.27
52.0		M. Taylor	(USA)	Philadelphia	4.7.28
	51.7 (51.67)	*R.Tisdall	(IRE)	Los Angeles	1.8.32
52.0n	(51.9)	G. Hardin	(USA)	Los Angeles	1.8.32
51.8		G. Hardin	(USA)	Milwaukee	30.6.34
50.6		G. Hardin	(USA)	Stockholm	26.7.34
50.4		Y. Lituyov	(URS)	Budapest	20.9.53
49.5		G. Davis	(USA)	Los Angeles	29.6.56
49.7y	(49.72y)	G. Potgieter	(SA)	Cardiff	22.7.58
49.2		G. Davis	(USA)	Budapest	6.8.58
49.3y		G. Potgieter	(SA)	Bloemfontein	16.4.60
49.2		S. Morale	(ITA)	Belgrade	14.9.62
49.1		W. Cawley	(USA)	Los Angeles	13.9.64
48.1	(48.94)	G. Vanderstock	(USA)	Echo Summit	11.9.68
48.1	(48.12)	D. Hemery	(GBR)	Mexico	15.10.68
47.8	(47.82)	J. Akii-Bua	(UGA)	Munich	2.9.72

Automatic Timing (Since May 1977)

47.82		J. Akii-Bua	(UGA)	Munich	2.9.72
47.64	(47.63)	E. Moses	(USA)	Montreal	25.7.76
47.45		E. Moses	(USA)	Westwood	11.6.77
47.13		E. Moses	(USA)	Milan	3.7.80
47.02		E. Moses	(USA)	Coblence	31.8.83

n = non winning performance
y = made at 440 yards
* = Tisdall's mark was not ratified as he knocked down a hurdle, and the record went to the second place winner.

100m HURDLES [WOMEN]

Best pre-IAAF performance

13.3h		P. Kilborn	(AUS)	Brisbane	13.3.69
13.3h		K. Balzer	(GDR)	Warsaw	20.6.69
13.3h		T. Sukniewicz	(POL)	Warsaw	20.6.69
13.0		K. Balzer	(GDR)	Leipzig	27.7.69
12.9		K. Balzer	(GDR)	Berlin	5.9.69
12.8		T. Sukniewicz	(POL)	Warsaw	20.6.70
12.8		C. Chi	(TPE)	Munich	12.7.70
12.7		K. Balzer	(GDR)	Berlin	26.7.70
12.7		T. Sukniewicz	(POL)	Warsaw	20.9.70
	12.7	T. Sukniewicz	(POL)	Erfurt	27.9.70
12.7		K. Balzer	(GDR)	Berlin	25.7.71
12.6		K. Balzer	(GDR)	Berlin	31.7.71
12.5		A. Ehrhardt	(GDR)	Potsdam	15.6.72
12.5		P. Kilborn-Ryan	(AUS)	Warsaw	28.6.72
	12.5	A. Ehrhardt	(GDR)	Berlin	13.8.72
12.3	(12.68)	A. Ehrhardt	(GDR)	Dresden	22.7.73

Automatic Timing (Since May 1977)

12.59		A. Ehrhardt	(GDR)	Munich	8.9.72
12.48		G. Rabsztyn	(POL)	Furth	10.6.78
	12.48	G. Rabsztyn	(POL)	Warsaw	18.6.79
12.36		G. Rabsztyn	(POL)	Warsaw	13.6.80
	12.36	Y. Donkova	(BUL)	Sofia	13.8.86
12.35		Y. Donkova	(BUL)	Cologne	17.8.86
12.29		Y. Donkova	(BUL)	Cologne	17.8.86
12.26		Y. Donkova	(BUL)	Ljubljana	7.9.86
12.25		G. Zagorcheva	(BUL)	Drama	8.7.87
12.21		Y. Donkova	(BUL)	Stara Zagora	20.8.88

400m HURDLES [WOMEN]

	61.1	S. Dyson	(GBR)	Bonn	15.5.71
	60.7	L. Macounova	(TCH)	Prague	29.7.72
	60.4	J. Vernon	(GBR)	London	21.3.73
	59.08	W. Koenig	(USA)	Phoenix	24.3.73
	58.6	M. Sykora	(AUT)	Warley	27.5.73
	57.3	M. Sykora	(AUT)	Frankfurt	23.6.73
	56.7	D. Piecyk	(POL)	Warsaw	11.8.73
56.5	(56.51)	K. Kacperczyk	(POL)	Augsburg	13.7.74
55.74		T. Storozheva	(URS)	Karl Marx Stadt	26.6.77
55.63		K. Rossley	(GDR)	Helsinki	13.8.77
55.44		K. Kacperczyk	(POL)	Berlin	18.8.78
55.31		T. Zelentsova	(URS)	Podolsk	19.8.78
54.89		T. Zelentsova	(URS)	Prague	2.9.78
54.78		M. Makeyeva	(URS)	Moscow	27.7.79
54.28		K. Rossley	(GDR)	Jena	17.5.80
54.02		A. Ambraziene	(URS)	Moscow	11.6.83
53.58		M. Ponomaryeva	(URS)	Kiev	22.6.84
53.55		S. Busch	(GDR)	Berlin	22.9.85
53.32		M. Stepanova	(URS)	Stuttgart	30.8.86
52.94		M. Stepanova	(URS)	Tashkent	17.9.86

UNITED KINGDOM RECORDS

MEN

110m HURDLES (y = 120y Hurdles)

16.0y	Clement Jackson	Oxford	14.11.65
16.0y	Samuel Palmer	Lillie Bridge	15.4.78
16.0y	Charles Daft	Stamford Bridge	3.7.86
16.0y	Dan Bulger	Stamford Bridge	2.7.92
15.8y	Dan Bulger	?	1.8.92
15.8y	Godfrey Shaw	Stamford Bridge	6.7.95
15.8y	Robert Stronach	Glasgow	29.7.05
15.6y	Kenneth Powell	Queen's Club	22.3.07
15.2y	Gerard Anderson	Stamford Bridge	11.5.12
15.2y	Fred Gaby	Stamford Bridge	7.6.23
15.2y	Fred Gaby	Stamford Bridge	18.7.25
15.1y	Fred Gaby	Stamford Bridge	3.7.26
14.8y	Lord Burghley	Cambridge	11.6.27
14.5y	Lord Burghley	Stamford Bridge	9.6.30
14.5	Don Finlay	Berlin	6.8.36
14.4	Don Finlay	Berlin	6.8.36
14.3	Don Finlay	Paris	4.9.38
14.3y	Jack Parker	London	30.7.55
14.3	Peter Hildreth	Hanover	15.9.57
14.3	Peter Hildreth	Oslo	26.8.58
14.3	Peter Hildreth	Gothenburg	28.8.58
14.3	Peter Hildreth	Paris	14.9.58
14.3y	Peter Hildreth	Cambridge	15.5.59
14.3	Peter Hildreth	Welwyn	9.7.60
14.3	Bob Birrell	London	13.8.60
14.3y	Mike Parker	Cambridge	4.5.61
14.3y	Bob Birrell	London	5.8.61
14.2	Mike Parker	Dortmund	3.9.61
14.2	Bob Birrell	Warsaw	6.9.61
14.0y (?w)	Bob Birrell	Welwyn	9.9.61
13.9	Mike Parker	Budapest	2.10.63
13.9	David Hemery	Odessa	3.7.66
13.9	Alan Pascoe	Szozecin	2.8.67
13.9	Alan Pascoe	Mexico City	16.10.68
13.9	Alan Pascoe	Rome	17.5.69
13.9	David Hemery	London	25.5.69
13.8	Alan Pascoe	Turin	2.6.69
13.6	David Hemery	Brno	5.7.69
13.6	David Hemery	Warsaw	13.9.70
13.5	Berwyn Price	Leipzig	1.7.73
13.5	Berwyn Price	Athens	14.5.76

Automatic Timing

13.74	David Hemery	Athens	20.9.69
13.72	David Hemery	Zurich	1.8.70
13.69	Berwyn Price	Moscow	18.8.73
13.68	Mark Holtom	London	9.6.82
13.66	Wilbert Greaves	Athens	2.9.82
13.60	Mark Holtom	London	17.9.82
13.43	Mark Holtom	Brisbane	4.10.82
13.41	Jon Ridgeon	London	2.8.87
13.36	Jon Ridgeon	London	12.8.87
13.29	Jon Ridgeon	Zagreb	15.7.87
13.29	Jon Ridgeon	Rome	3.9.87
13.23	Colin Jackson	Belfast	27.6.88
13.11	Colin Jackson	Sestriere	11.8.88
13.11	Colin Jackson	London	13.7.89
13.11	Colin Jackson	Auckland	27.1.90
13.08	Colin Jackson	Auckland	28.1.90

400m HURDLES (y = 440y H time)

57.2y	Godfrey Shaw	Douglas	12.8.91
56.8y	Gerard Anderson	Stamford Bridge	16.7.10
56.0y	Frederick Blackett	Stamford Bridge	17.7.25
55.6y	Lord Burghley	Stamford Bridge	2.7.26
55.0y	Lord Burghley	Stamford Bridge	3.7.26
54.2y	Lord Burghley	Stamford Bridge	2.7.27
54.0y	Lord Burghley	Stamford Bridge	3.7.28
54.0	T. L. Learmonth	Amsterdam	29.7.28
53.4	Lord Burghley	Amsterdam	30.7.28
53.0	Lord Burghley	Los Angeles	31.7.32
52.2	Lord Burghley	Los Angeles	1.8.32
51.5	Harry Kane	London	13.10.54
51.1	Tom Farrell	London	23.8.57
51.0	Tom Farrell	London	13.6.60
51.0	Chris Surety	Dortmund	2.9.61
51.0	John Cooper	London	14.8.63
50.5	John Cooper	Volgograd	29.9.63
50.5	John Cooper	Tokyo	14.10.64
50.4	John Cooper	Tokyo	15.10.64
50.1	John Cooper	Tokyo	16.10.64
49.8	David Hemery	Berkeley	15.6.68
49.6	David Hemery	London	24.8.68
49.3	John Sherwood	Mexico City	14.10.68
49.3	David Hemery	Mexico City	14.10.68

Automatic Timing

52.01	Lord Burghley	Los Angeles	1.8.32
51.85	Harry Kane	Melbourne	23.11.56
51.52	Mike Hogan	Porto Alegre	7.9.63
50.58	John Cooper	Tokyo	14.10.64

50.40	John Cooper	Tokyo	15.10.64
50.19	John Cooper	Tokyo	16.10.64
49.37	John Sherwood	Mexico City	14.10.68
49.37	David Hemery	Mexico City	14.10.68
48.12	David Hemery	Mexico City	15.10.68
47.92	Kriss Akabusi	Split	29.8.90
47.91	Kriss Akabusi	Tokyo	26.8.91
47.86	Kriss Akabusi	Tokyo	27.8.91

WOMEN
100m HURDLES

13.7	Chris Bell	Blackburn	3.6.67
13.7	Chris Bell	London	19.7.68
13.5	Chris Bell	London	19.7.68
13.4	Chris Bell	Berlin	2.8.70
13.4	Judy Vernon	Zurich	20.5.72
13.2	Judy Vernon	Helsinki	26.7.72
13.2	Judy Vernon	Bucharest	9.6.74
13.2	Judy Vernon	Warsaw	22.6.74
13.0	Judy Vernon	Warsaw	29.6.74
13.0	Blondelle Thompson	Warsaw	29.6.74

Automatic Timing

13.29	Mary Peters	Munich	2.9.72
13.21	Sharon Colyear	Bydgoszcz	22.6.76
13.11	Sharon Colyear	Bydgoszcz	22.6.76
13.08	Lorna Booth	London	11.6.78
13.06	Shirley Strong	Stuttgart	11.7.80
13.06	Shirley Strong	London	30.7.83
12.95	Shirley Strong	London	30.7.83
12.91	Shirley Strong	Helsinki	12.8.83
12.87	Shirley Strong	Zurich	24.8.83
12.82	Sally Gunnell	Zurich	17.8.88

400m HURDLES

61.1	Sandra Dyson	Bonn	15.5.71
60.4	Judy Vernon	London	21.3.73
60.3	Christine Warden	Warley	27.5.73
59.87	Judy Vernon	London	14.9.73
58.86	Christine Warden	London	26.5.74
58.0	Christine Warden	Warsaw	30.6.74
57.84	Christine Warden	London	21.8.76
57.6	Christine Warden	Cwmbran	11.6.77
57.59	Liz Sutherland	Edinburgh	25.8.77
57.0	Christine Warden	Cleckheaton	20.5.78
56.80	Christine Warden	Bremen	23.6.79
56.06	Christine Warden	London	28.7.79
56.04	Sue Morley	Helsinki	10.8.83

55.40	Sally Gunnell	Birmingham	6.8.88
55.00	Sally Gunnell	London	28.8.88
54.48	Sally Gunnell	Seoul	26.9.88
54.03	Sally Gunnell	Seoul	28.9.88
53.78	Sally Gunnell	Monte Carlo	3.8.91
53.61	Sally Gunnell	Zurich	7.8.91
53.16	Sally Gunnell	Tokyo	29.8.91

Kay Morley, Commonwealth 100m Hurdles Champion 1990.

Sally Gunnell, Commonwealth 400m Hurdles Champion 1990 and Silver Medallist at World Championships 1991.

Colin Jackson, Olympic 110m Hurdles Silver Medallist 1988, Commonwealth and European Champion 1990.

Kriss Akabusi, Commonwealth and European 400m Hurdles Champion 1990 and Bronze Medallist at World Championships 1991.

71

NOTES